lon

Fast Talk

# Danish

Guaranteed to get you talking

T0011748

# Contents

## ⇒ Special Features

# *Before You Go*

*Many visitors to Denmark get around without speaking a word of Danish, but just a few phrases go a long way in making friends, inviting service with a smile, and ensuring a rich and rewarding travel experience – you could be invited in for some hygge, experience a sublime meal, or grab that great shopping bargain.*

Danish belongs to the North Germanic language group, together with Swedish, Norwegian, Icelandic and Faeroese. Consequently, written Danish bears a strong resemblance to these languages. Spoken Danish, on the other hand, has evolved in a different direction, introducing sounds and pronunciation not found elsewhere.

## PRONUNCIATION TIPS

Danish varies from island to island as well as from north to south, with each region having its distinct dialect. The translation and pronunciation presented here follows the form of Danish known as Nudansk, (literally 'Now Danish'). This is the form of Danish spoken in Copenhagen, and understood throughout the country.

Stressed syllables in multi-syllable words are printed here in italic type, and longer syllables have been split into more manageable lengths.

Danes do not necessarily pronounce what they write. The pronunciation of letters varies depending on the word, and written vowels and/or consonants will sometimes 'disappear' completely in the pronunciation. Unfortunately there are no hard and fast rules as to how any given letter is to be pronounced. In general, the best advice for good pronunciation is to listen and learn. Good luck!

See page 12 for our pronunciation guide.

## MUST-KNOW GRAMMAR

Danish has a polite form of address, using the personal pronouns De and Dem. The words and phrases in this book are mostly in the familar form using du and dig, except where it's more appropriate to use the formal form. In general, use the formal form when speaking to senior citizens and officials, and the familiar form the rest of the time.

# Fast Talk Danish

Don't worry if you've never learnt Danish (*dansk* dansk) before – it's all about confidence. You don't need to memorise endless grammatical details or long lists of vocabulary – you just need to start speaking. You have nothing to lose and everything to gain when the locals hear you making an effort. And remember that body language and a sense of humour have a role to play in every culture.

*"you just need to start speaking"*

Even if you use the very basics, such as greetings and civilities, your travel experience will be the better for it. Once you start, you'll be amazed how many prompts you'll get to help you build on those first words. You'll hear people speaking, pick up sounds and expressions from the locals, catch a word or two that you know from TV already, see something on a billboard – all these things help to build your understanding.

5

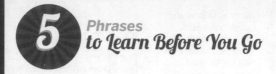

# 5 Phrases to Learn Before You Go

**1.** **What are the opening hours?**
**Hvad er åbningstiderne?**
va ehr *åb*-neengs-tee-thah-nah

Opening hours vary throughout the year, especially for sights and activities.

**2.** **Thanks for the meal.**
**Tak for mad.**
taht for math

After a meal you should always say tak for mad before getting up.

**3.** **Which wine would you recommend?**
**Hvilken vin anbefaler du?**
vil-*gehn* veen *an*-beh-fah-lah doo

When Danes raise their glasses to you and say Skål! it means 'Cheers!'

**4.** **Can I address you with 'du'?**
**Må jeg sige du?**
må yai *see*-yeh doo

Danes generally only use the familiar form of address (du and dig) for everyone but senior citizens and officials.

**5.** **Do you have plans for tonight?**
**Har du planer i aften?**
hah doo *pla*-nah ee *ahf*-den

Danish kitchens close relatively early: aim to eat before 10pm, before 9pm or earlier in smaller towns.

## 10 Phrases to Sound Like a Local

| Cool! | Cool! | kool |
|---|---|---|
| No worries. | Ikke noget problem. | ig *nā*-eht *pror*-blehm |
| Sure. | Selvfølgelig. | seh-*fer*-lee |
| No way! | No way! | nāw way |
| Just joking! | Jeg laver bare fis! | yai *la*-vah bah fees |
| Too bad. | Bare ærgerligt | bah *ehr*-wa-leet |
| What a shame. | Sikke en skam. | *sig*-geh in sgahm |
| What's up? | Hvad sker der? | va sgeh dah |
| Well done! | Flot klaret! | flāt *klah*-eht |
| Not bad. | Ikke dårligt. | ig *dā*-leet |

# 10 Phrases to Start a Sentence

| | |
|---|---|
| **When is (the next flight)?** | Hvornår går (næste fly)? <br> vor-*nor* gor *nehs*-deh flü |
| **Where is (the station)?** | Hvor er (station)? <br> vor ehŕ (sda-*shorn*) |
| **Where can I (buy a ticket)?** | Hvor kan jeg (købe en billet)? <br> vor ka yai (*ker*-beh in bi-*leht*) |
| **Do you have (a light)?** | Har du (ild)? <br> hah doo il |
| **Is there (a toilet)?** | Er der (toilet)? <br> ehŕ dehŕ (toy-*leht*) |
| **I'd like (a coffee).** | Jeg vil gerne have (kaffe). <br> yai vi *gehŕ*-neh ha (*kah*-feh) |
| **I'd like to (return this).** | Jeg vil gerne (returnere dette). <br> yai vi *gehŕ*-neh (*reh*-tooh-ni-ah *di*-deh) |
| **Can I (enter)?** | Må jeg (komme ind)? <br> mā yai (*kom*-eh in) |
| **Do I have to (book a seat)?** | Er det nødvendigt at (bestille plads)? <br> ehŕ di nerth-vehn-deet at (bi-*sdi*-leh plas) |
| **Can you (write down the price)?** | Kan du (skrive prisen)? <br> ka doo (*sgree*-veh pree-*sehn*) |

8

# Chatting & Basics

## ≡ Fast Phrases

| Hello. | Hej/Dav/Goddag. inf/pol |
|---|---|
| | hai/dow/gor-da |
| **Thank you.** | Tak. |
| | tahk |
| **Do you speak English?** | Taler De engelsk? pol |
| | *ta*-lah dee *ehng*-ehlsk |

## Essentials

| Goodbye. | Hej hej/Farvel. inf/pol |
|---|---|
| | hai hai/fah-*vehl* |
| **Yes./No.** | Ja./Nej. |
| | ya/nai |
| **Excuse me.** | Undskyld. |
| | *ān*-sgül |
| **May I? Do you mind?** | Må jeg? Tillader De? pol |
| | må yai? *ti*-la-thah dee |
| **Sorry. (excuse me, forgive me)** | Undskyld/Beklager. |
| | *ān*-sgül/bi-*kla*-ah |
| **Many thanks.** | Mange tak. |
| | *mahng*-eh tahg |
| **That's fine. You're welcome.** | Det er i orden. Selv tak. |
| | di ehr ee *or*dehn. sehl tahk |

## Language Difficulties

| | |
|---|---|
| **Do you speak English?** | Taler De engelsk? pol<br>*ta*-lah dee *ehng*-ehlsk |
| **Does anyone speak English?** | Er der nogen der taler engelsk?<br>ehr dah norn dah *ta*-lah *ehng*-ehlsk |
| **I speak a little ...** | Jeg taler en smule ...<br>yai *ta*-lah in *smoo*-leh ... |
| **I don't speak ...** | Jeg taler ikke ...<br>yai *ta*-lah ig ... |
| **I (don't) understand.** | Jeg forstår (ikke).<br>yai fo-*sdor* (ig) |
| **Could you repeat that?** | Kunne De gentage det? pol<br>*koo*-neh dee *gehn*-ta di |
| **Could you speak more slowly please?** | Kunne De tale langsommere? pol<br>*koo*-neh dee *ta*-leh *lahng*-som-ah |
| **How do you say ...?** | Hvordan siger man ...?<br>vor-*dan see*-ah man ... |
| **What does ... mean?** | Hvad betyder ...?<br>va bi-*tüth*-ah ... |

## Greetings

| | |
|---|---|
| **Good morning.** | Godmorgen.<br>gor-*morn* |
| **Good afternoon.** | God eftermiddag.<br>gor *ehf*-dah-mi-da |
| **Good evening/night.** | Godaften./Godnat.<br>gor-*ahf*-dehn/gor-*nat* |
| **How are you?** | Hvordan går det?<br>vor-*dan* gor di |
| **Well, thanks.** | Godt, tak.<br>got tahk |

**Fast Talk**

### Pretty Please

Note that there is no equivalent to the word 'please' in Danish. Politeness is most often expressed by tone of voice and/or by beginning the sentence with phrases such as 'May I ...' Må jeg ... or 'Could I ...' Kunne jeg ....

## Titles

| | |
|---|---|
| **Madam/Mrs** | fru |
| | *froo* |
| **Sir/Mr** | herr (hr.) |
| | *hehr* |
| **Miss** | frøken |
| | *ffer-gehn* |

## Introductions

| | |
|---|---|
| **What is your name?** | Hvad hedder du/De? inf/pol |
| | va *hi*-thah doo/dee |
| **My name is ...** | Mit navn er ... |
| | mid naown ehr ... |
| **I'm pleased to meet you.** | Det er hyggeligt at træffe Dern/møde dig. pol/inf |
| | di ehr *hüg*-lit at *trah*-feh dehm/*mer*-theh dai |
| **I'd like to introduce you to ...** | Jeg vil gerne præsentere dig for ... |
| | yai vi *gehr*-neh prehsehn-*ti*-ah dai for ... |
| ✂ **Sure.** | Selvfølgelig./Det er klart. |
| | seh-*fer*-lee/di ehr klaht |

11

## Pronunciation

Below is a general pronunciation guide of Danish sounds, outlining in red our representation of each sound used in the simplified transliterations throughout the book. Consonants not listed here are pronounced as in English.

Stressed syllables in multi-syllable words are printed here in italic type, and longer syllables have been split into more manageable lengths.

The stress is usually placed on the first syllable, or on the first letter of the word.

Vowels

| | |
|---|---|
| ah | as the 'a' in 'father' |
| uh | as the 'u' in 'cut' |
| a | as the 'a' in 'act' |
| ā | a long rounded 'a' as in 'walk' |
| eh | as the 'e' in 'bet' |
| ee | as the 'ee' in 'seethe' |
| i | as the 'i' in 'hit' |
| ü | a bit like the 'e' in British English 'dew' – try pursing your lips and saying 'ee' |
| o | a short 'o' as in 'pot' |
| oh | as the 'o' in 'note' |
| oo | a long 'oo' as in 'cool' |
| u | a short 'oo' as in 'foot' |
| ö | as the 'e' in 'summer' |
| or | as the 'or' in 'for', with less emphasis on the 'r' |
| er | as the 'er' in 'fern' but shorter, without the 'r' |

### Diphthongs

| | |
|---|---|
| ae | as the 'ea' in 'bear' |
| ay | as the 'ay' in 'day' |
| ai | as the sound of 'eye' |
| oy | the 'oy' as in 'toy' |
| ow | as the 'ou' in 'out' |

### Semiconsonants

| | |
|---|---|
| w | as in 'wet' |
| y | as in 'yet' |

### Consonants

| | |
|---|---|
| s | always as in 'kiss', never as in 'treasure' |
| sh | as in 'ship' |
| ch | as in 'chew' |
| dj | as the 'j' in 'jaw' |
| th | as the 'th' in 'lather' |
| h | as the 'h' in 'horse' |
| ng | as in 'sing' |
| ngn | as the meeting of sounds in 'hang-nail' |
| ŕ | rolled in the throat |
| rr | a trilled 'r' |
| rt | as the 'rt' in American English 'start' |
| rd | as the 'rd' in American English 'weird' |
| rn | as the 'rn' in American English 'earn' |
| rl | as the 'rl' in American English 'earl' |
| dn | as the 'dn' in 'hadn't' |
| dl | as the 'dl' in 'saddle' |

**Starting Off**

When starting to speak another language, your biggest hurdle is saying aloud what may seem to be just a bunch of sounds. The best way to do this is to memorise a few key words, like 'hello', 'thank you' and 'how much?', plus at least one phrase that's not essential, eg 'how are you', 'see you later' or 'it's very cold/hot' (people love to talk about the weather!). This will enable you to make contact with the locals, and when you get a reply and a smile, it'll also boost your confidence.

## Personal Details

| Where are you from? | Hvor kommer du fra? |
|---|---|
| | vor *kom*-ah doo *frah* |

PHRASE BUILDER

| I'm from ... | Jeg er fra ... | yai ehŕ fŕah ... |
|---|---|---|
| Australia | Australien | ow-*sdŕahl*-yehn |
| Canada | Kanada | *ka*-na-da |
| England | England | *ehng*-lan |
| New Zealand | New Zealand | nü *si*-lan |
| the USA | USA | oo ehs a |

## Age

| How old are you? | Hvor gammel er du? |
|---|---|
| | vor *gah*-mehl ehŕ doo |
| I'm ... years old. | Jeg er ... år gammel. |
| | yai ehŕ ... or *gah*-mehl |

## PHRASE BUILDER

| I'm ... | Jeg er ... | yai ehŕ ... |
|---|---|---|
| **married** | gift | geeft |
| **single** | ugift | oo-geeft |

# Occupations & Study

| What do you do? | Hvad laver du?<br>va *la*-wah doo |
|---|---|

## PHRASE BUILDER

| I'm (a/an) ... | Jeg er ... | yai ehŕ ... |
|---|---|---|
| I work as (a/an) ... | Jeg arbejder som ... | yai *ah*-bai-dah som ... |
| **doctor** | læge | *leh*-eh |
| **farmer** | bonde | *bā*-neh |
| **journalist** | journalist | shor-na-*list* |
| **lawyer** | advokat | ath-vor-*kat* |
| **nurse** | sygeplejerske | *sü*-eh-plai-yah-sheh |
| **office worker** | kontorarbejder | kon-*tooŕ*-ah-bai-dah |
| **student** | studerende | sdoo-*di*-ah-neh |
| **teacher** | lærer | *lehŕ*-ah |
| **waiter** | tjener | *cheh*-nah |

| This is my ... | Dette er min ... | *di*-deh ehf meen ... |
|---|---|---|
| brother | bror | *bfof* |
| daughter | datter | *da*-tah |
| husband | mand | man |
| sister | søster | *sers*-dah |
| son | søn | sern |
| wife | kone | *kor*-ne |

## Interests

| What do you do in your spare time? | Hvad laver du i din fritid? inf<br>va *la*-wah doo ee deen *free*-teeth |
|---|---|
| art | kunst<br>kānst |
| cooking | madlavning<br>math-laow-ning |
| fishing | fiskeri<br>fis-gah-*fee* |
| going out | gå i byen<br>gor ee *bü*-ehn |
| going to the cinema | gå i biografen<br>gor ee bee-or-*gfahf*-ehn |
| music | musik<br>moo-*seek* |
| photography | fotografering<br>for-tor-gfah-*fi*-fing |
| reading | læse<br>*leh*-seh |
| shopping | handle<br>*han*-leh |

| sport | sport |
| | sbort |
| **the theatre** | teatret |
| | ti-*a*-tŕaht |
| **travelling** | rejse |
| | *ŕai*-seh |
| **writing** | skrive |
| | *sgŕee*-weh |

## Feelings

| I like ... | Jeg kan godt lide ... |
| | yai ka got lee ... |
| I don't like ... | Jeg kan ikke lide ... |
| | yai ka ig lee ... |

### PHRASE BUILDER

| I'm ... | Jeg er ... | yai ehŕ ... |
|---|---|---|
| **angry** | vred | vŕehth |
| **cold** | fryser | frü-sah |
| **happy** | glad | glath |
| **hot** | sveder | svith-ah |
| **hungry** | sulten | *sul*-dehn |
| **sad** | trist | tŕeest |
| **sleepy** | søvnig | *serv*-nee |
| **thirsty** | tørstig | *ters*-dee |
| **tired (fatigued)** | træt | tŕaht |
| **well** | har det godt | hah di got |

## Numbers

| | | |
|---|---|---|
| 0 | nul | nāl |
| 1 | en | in |
| 2 | to | tor |
| 3 | tre | tŕeh |
| 4 | fire | feeŕ |
| 5 | fem | fehm |
| 6 | seks | sehks |
| 7 | syv | sü-w |
| 8 | otte | *or*-deh |
| 9 | ni | nee |
| 10 | ti | tee |
| 11 | elve | *ehl*-veh |
| 12 | tolv | tol |
| 13 | tretten | *tŕah*-dehn |
| 14 | fjorten | *fyor*-dehn |
| 15 | femten | *fehm*-dehn |
| 16 | seksten | *sais*-dehn |
| 17 | sytten | *ser*-dehn |
| 18 | atten | *a*-dehn |
| 19 | nitten | *ni*-dehn |
| 20 | tyve | *tü*-weh |
| 21 | enogtyve | *in*-o-tü-weh |
| 30 | tredive | *tŕahth*-veh |
| 40 | fyrre | *feŕ*-eh |
| 50 | halvtreds | hal-*tŕehs* |
| 60 | tres | tŕehs |
| 70 | halvfjerds | hal-*fyehŕs* |

| 80 | firs | feeŕs |
| 90 | halvfems | hal-*fehms* |
| 100 | hundrede | *hoon*-ahth |
| 1000 | tusind | *too*-sehn |
| **one million** | en million | in mee-lee-*orn* |

## Time

| What time is it? | Hvad er klokken?<br>va ehŕ *klog*-gehn |
|---|---|
| It's ... am/pm. | Klokken er ... om morgenen/<br>aftenen.<br>*klog*-gehn ehŕ ... om *mor*-nehn/<br>*ahfd*-nehn |
| **in the morning** | om morgenen<br>om *mor*-nehn |
| **in the afternoon** | om eftermiddagen<br>om *ehf*-dah-mi-da-ehn |
| **in the evening** | om aftenen<br>om *ahfd*-nehn |

## Days

| **Monday** | mandag | *man*-da |
| **Tuesday** | tirsdag | *teeŕs*-da |
| **Wednesday** | onsdag | *ǎns*-da |
| **Thursday** | torsdag | *toŕs*-da |
| **Friday** | fredag | *ffreh*-da |
| **Saturday** | lørdag | *ler*-da |
| **Sunday** | søndag | *sern*-da |

## Months

| English | Danish | Pronunciation |
|---|---|---|
| January | januar | *yan*-oo-ah |
| February | februar | *feb*-froo-ah |
| March | marts | mahts |
| April | april | a-*preel* |
| May | maj | mai |
| June | juni | *yoo*-nee |
| July | juli | *yoo*-lee |
| August | august | ow-*gäst* |
| September | september | sib-*tehm*-bah |
| October | oktober | org-*tor*-bah |
| November | november | nor-*vehm*-bah |
| December | december | di-*sehm*-bah |

## Seasons

| English | Danish | Pronunciation |
|---|---|---|
| summer | sommer | *som*-ah |
| autumn | efterår | *ehf*-dah-or |
| winter | vinter | *vin*-dah |
| spring | forår | *for*-or |

## Dates

| | |
|---|---|
| What date is it today? | Hvilken dato er det i dag? *vil*-gehn *da*-toh ehr di ee da |
| today | i dag ee da |
| this morning | i morges ee *mor*-ehs |

| tonight | i nat |
| | ee nat |
| this week | denne uge |
| | *dehn*-neh *oo*-eh |
| this year | i år |
| | ee or |
| yesterday | i går |
| | ee gor |
| yesterday morning | i går morges |
| | ee gor *mor*-ehs |
| last night | i (går) nat; i (går) aftes |
| | ee (gor) nat; ee (gor) *ahf*-dehs |
| last week | forrige uge |
| | *for*-ee *oo*-eh |
| last year | sidste år |
| | *sees*-deh or |
| tomorrow | i morgen |
| | ee *mor*-wen |
| next week | næste uge |
| | *nehs*-deh *oo*-eh |
| next year | næste år |
| | *nehs*-deh or |
| afternoon | eftermiddag |
| | *ehf*-dah-mi-da |
| day | dag |
| | da |
| early | tidlig |
| | *teeth*-lee |
| midnight | midnat |
| | *meeth*-nat |
| morning | morgen |
| | *mor*-wen |

| night | nat |
| | nat |
| noon | middagstid |
| | *mi*-das-teeth |

## Weather

| What's the weather like? | Hvordan er vejret? |
| | vor-*dan* ehŕ *vehŕ*-eht |
| It's ... today. | Det er ... i dag. |
| | di ehŕ ... ee da |

PHRASE BUILDER

| Will it be ... tomorrow? | Bliver det ... i morgen? | bleer di ... ee morn? |
|---|---|---|
| cloudy | overskyet | *ow*-ah-sgü-ehtt |
| cold | koldt | kolt |
| hot | varmt | vahmt |
| raining | regnvejr | *fain*-vehŕ |
| snowing | snevejr | sni-vehŕ |
| sunny | solskinsvejr | *sorl*-sgins-vehŕ |
| windy | blæsevejr | *bleh*-seh-vehŕ |

## Directions

| Where is ...? | Hvor er ...? |
| | vor ehŕ ... |
| How do I get to ...? | Hvordan kommer jeg til ...? |
| | vor-dan kom-ah yai ti ... |
| Is it far from here? | Er det langt herfra? |
| | ehŕ di lahngt *hiŕ-ffah* |

| | | |
|---|---|---|
| **Can I walk there?** | Kan jeg gå derhen? | |
| | ka yai *gå* dah-*hehn* | |
| **Can you show me (on the map)?** | Kunne De/du vise mig det (på kortet)? **pol/inf** | |
| | koo-neh dee/doo *vee*-seh mai di (på *kort*-eht) | |
| **Are there other means of getting there?** | Er der andre måder at komme derhen på? | |
| | ehr dehr *ahn*-drah *måth*-ah at *kom*-eh dehr-*hehn* på | |
| **I want to go to ...** | Jeg vil gerne til ... | |
| | yai vi *gehr*-neh ti ... | |
| **Go straight ahead.** | Gå lige ud. | |
| | gå *li*-eh óoth | |
| **behind** | bag | |
| | ba | |
| **far** | fjern | |
| | fyehŕn | |
| **near** | nær | |
| | nehŕ | |
| **opposite** | på den modsatte side af | |
| | på dehn *morth*-sa-deh *see*-theh a | |

---

### PHRASE BUILDER

| | | |
|---|---|---|
| **Turn left/ right ...** | Drej til venstre/ højre ... | dŕai ti *vehns*-dŕah/ *hoy*-yah ... |
| **at the next corner** | ved næste hjørne | vi *nehs*-deh *yer*-neh |
| **at the traffic lights** | ved trafiklyset | vi tŕah-*feeg*-lü-sehth |

# Airport & Transport

## Fast Phrases

| | |
|---|---|
| **What time is the next bus?** | Hvornår går den næste bus? <br> vor-*nor* gor dehn *nehs*-deh boos |
| **Does this train go to ...?** | Går dette tog til ...? <br> gor *di*-deh tāw ti ... |
| **I'd like to book a seat to ...** | Jeg vil gerne bestille plads til ... <br> yai vi *gehŕ*-neh bi-*sdi*-leh plas ti ... |

## Getting Around

| | |
|---|---|
| **What time does the ... leave/arrive?** | Hvornår går/ankommer ... <br> vor-*nor* gor/*an*-kom-ah ... |
| **(aero)plane** | flyet <br> *flü*-eht |
| **boat** | båden <br> *bā*-thehn |
| **bus** | bussen/rutebilen <br> *boo*-sehn/*roo*-deh-*bee*-lehn |
| **train** | toget <br> *tā*-weht |

## At the Airport

| | |
|---|---|
| **Is there a flight to ...?** | Er der et fly til ...? <br> ehŕ dehŕ it flü ti ... |

| When is the next flight to ...? | Hvornår går næste fly til ...?<br>*vor-nor* gor *nehs*-deh flü ti ... |
|---|---|
| How long does the flight take? | Hvor lang tid tager flyveturen?<br>vor lahng tith tah *flü*-weh-too-ahn |
| What is the flight number? | Hvad er flight-nummeret?<br>va ehŕ *flait*-nām-mahth |
| You must check in at ... (time) | Du skal checke ind klokken ...<br>doo sga *cheh*-geh in *klog*-gehn ... |
| airport tax | lufthavnsskal<br>*lāfd*-hown-skat |
| boarding pass | boardingkort<br>*boŕ*-ding-kort |
| customs | told<br>tol |

## 🔍 LOOK FOR

| | |
|---|---|
| BAGAGE(AFHENTNING) | LUGGAGE PICKUP |
| BAGAGE(SKRANKE) | BAGGAGE COUNTER |
| CHECK IN/<br>INDCHEKNING | CHECKING IN |
| CHECK-IN (SKRANKE) | CHECK-IN COUNTER |
| REGISTRERING | REGISTRATION |
| TOLD | CUSTOMS |

## Buying Tickets

| Where can I buy a ticket? | Hvor kan jeg købe en billet?<br>vor ka yai *ker*-beh in bi-*leht* |
|---|---|
| I want to go to ... | Jeg vil gerne til ...<br>yai vi *gehŕ*-neh ti ... |

25

| | | |
|---|---|---|
| **Do I need to book?** | Er det nødvendigt at bestille plads? | ehř di nerth-*vehn*-deed at bi-*sdi*-leh plas |
| **I'd like to book a seat to ...** | Jeg vil gerne bestille plads til ... | yai vi *gehř*-neh bi-*sdi*-leh plas ti ... |
| **It's full.** | Det er fuldt booket. | di ehř *foolt book*-eht |
| **Are there no seats available at all?** | Er der slet ingen ledige pladser? | ehř dah slehd *ing*-ehn le-thee plas-ah |

---

### PHRASE BUILDER

| **I'd like ...** | Jeg vil gerne have ... | yai vi *gehř*-neh ha ... |
|---|---|---|
| **a one-way ticket** | en enkelt-billet | en *ehng*-gehlt-bi-leht |
| **a return ticket** | en returbillet | en řeh-*toof*-bi-leht |
| **two tickets** | to billetter | tor bi-*lehd*-ah |
| **tickets for all of us** | billetter til os alle | bi-*lehd*-ah ti os *al*-eh |
| **a student discount** | studenter-rabat | sdoo-*dehn*-dah-řah-bat |
| **a child's fare** | en børnebillet | in *ber*-neh-bi-leht |
| **a pensioner's fare** | en pensionist-billet | in pahng-sho-*neest*-bi-leht |
| **1st class** | første klasse | *fers*-deh *klas*-eh |
| **2nd class** | anden klasse | *an*-ehn *klas*-eh |

| Can I get a stand-by ticket? | Kan jeg måske købe en stand-by billet? |
| | ka yai mās-keh ker-beh in stan-bai bi-leht |

## Bus & Train

| Where is the bus stop? | Hvor er busstoppestedet? |
| | vor ehr boos-stop-peh-stehth-eht |
| Which bus goes to ...? | Hvilken bus går til ...? |
| | vil-gehn boos gor ti ... |
| Does this bus go to ...? | Går denne bus til ...? |
| | gor dehn-neh boos ti ... |
| How often do buses pass by? | Hvor ofte går bussen? |
| | vor of-deh gor boos-sen |
| Could you let me know when we get to ...? | Kunne De/du sige til når vi kommer til ...? pol/inf |
| | koo-neh dee/doo see-yeh ti nor vee kom-ah ti ... |
| I want to get off! | Jeg vil af! |
| | yai vi a! |
| Which line takes me to ...? | Hvilket tog går til ...? |
| | vil-geht tāw gor ti ... |
| What is the next station? | Hvad er næste station? |
| | va ehr nehs-deh sda-shorn |
| Is this the right platform for ...? | Er dette den rigtige perron når jeg skal med toget til ...? |
| | ehr di-deh dehn rig-dee pa-rong nor yai sga meh tā-weht ti ... |
| The train leaves from platform ... | Toget går fra perron ... |
| | tā-weht gor ffah pa-rong ... |
| Passengers must change trains/platforms. | Passagererne skal skifte tog/perron. |
| | pa-sa-shi-ah-neh sga sgeef-deh tāw/pa-rong |

27

| dining car | spisevogn |
| | *sbee*-seh-vown |
| express | ekspres |
| | ehgs-*prahs* |
| local | lokal |
| | lor-*kal* |
| sleeping car | sovevogn |
| | *sow*-eh-vown |

PHRASE BUILDER

| What time is the ... bus? | Hvornår går den ... bus? | vor-*nor* gor dehn ... boos |
|---|---|---|
| next | næste | *nehs*-deh |
| first | første | *fers*-deh |
| last | sidste | *sees*-deh |

## Taxi

| Can you take me to ...? | Kan De/du køre mig til ...? pol/inf |
| | ka dee/doo *ker*-re mai ti ... |
| How much does it cost to go to ...? | Hvor meget koster det at køre til ...? |
| | vor *mah*-eth kos-dah di at *ker*-re ti ... |
| Here is fine, thank you. | Stop her, tak. |
| | sdop hehr tahk |
| The next corner, please. | Ved næste hjørne, tak. |
| | vi *nehs*-deh *yer*-neh tahk |
| The next street to the left/right. | Næste gade til venstre/højre. |
| | *nehs*-deh ga-theh ti *vehns*-drah/*hoy*-yah |
| Please slow down. | Vær så venlig at køre langsommere. |
| | vehr so *vehn*-lee at *ker*-re *lahng*-som-ah |

| Continue! | Fortsæt!<br>*fofd*-seht |
| --- | --- |
| Stop here! | Stop her!<br>sdop hehf |
| Please wait here. | Vent venligst her.<br>vehnt *vehn*-leest hehf |

## Car & Motorbike

| Where can I rent a car? | Hvor kan jeg leje en bil?<br>vor ka yai *lai*-eh in beel |
| --- | --- |
| How much is it daily/weekly? | Hvor meget koster det per dag/<br>per uge?<br>vor *mah*-eth *kos*-dah di pehf da/<br>pehf *oo*-eh |
| Does that include insurance/ mileage? | Inkluderer det forsikring/<br>ubegrænsede kilometer?<br>ing-kloo-*di*-ah di fo-*sig*-fing/<br>oo-bi-gfahn-seh-theh kee-lor-*mi*-dah |
| Where's the next petrol station? | Hvor er næste benzinstation?<br>vor ehf *nehs*-deh bin-*seen*-sda-*shorn*? |
| How long can I park here? | Hvor længe må jeg parkere her?<br>vor *lehng*-eh må yai pah-*ki*-ah hehf |
| Does this road lead to ...? | Fører denne vej til ...?<br>*fef*-ah *dehn* neh vai ti ... |
| I need a mechanic. | Jeg har brug for en mekaniker.<br>yai hah bfoo for in mi-*ka*-ni-gah |
| What make is it? | Hvilket mærke er det?<br>*vil*-geht *mehf*-geh ehf di |
| The battery is flat. | Batteriet er dødt.<br>ba-dah-*fee*-eht ehf dert |
| The radiator is leaking. | Køleren er utæt.<br>*ker*-lahn ehf *oo*-teht |

| I have a flat tyre. | Jeg er punkteret. |
| | yai ehŕ pāng-*ti*-ahth |
| It's overheating. (engine) | Motoren koger over. |
| | *mor*-toŕ-ahn *koh*-wah *ow*-ah |
| It's not working. | Den virker ikke. |
| | dehn *veeŕ*-gah ig |

## Useful Phrases

| The train is delayed/cancelled. | Toget er forsinket/aflyst. |
| | *tāw*-eht ehŕ for-*sing*-geht/*ow*-lüst |
| How long will it be delayed? | Hvor meget er toget forsinket? |
| | vor *mai*-yeht ehŕ *tāw*-eht fo-*sing*-geht |
| Can I reserve a place? | Er det muligt at reservere plads? |
| | ehŕ di *moo*-lit at ŕeh-sehŕ-*vi*-ah plas |
| How long does the trip take? | Hvor lang tid tager turen? |
| | vor lahng teeth tah *too*-ahn |
| Is it a direct route? | Er det en direkte forbindelse? |
| | ehŕ di in *dee*-ŕaig-deh fo-*bin*-ehl-seh |
| Is that seat taken? | Er den plads optaget? |
| | ehŕ dehn plas *ob*-ta-eht |
| I want to get off at ... | Jeg vil gerne af ved ... |
| | yai vi *gehŕ*-neh a vi ... |
| Where can I hire a bicycle? | Hvor kan jeg leje en cykel? |
| | vor ka yai *lai*-eh in *sü*-gehl |

# Accommodation

## Fast Phrases

| I have a reservation. | Jeg har en reservation. *yai hah in reh-sah-vah-syorn* |
| When/where is breakfast served? | Hvornår/hvor er der morgenmad? *vor-nor/vor ehr dah morn-math* |
| What time is checkout? | Hvad tid er checkout? *va teeth ehr chehk-owt* |

## Finding Accommodation

| What's the address? | Hvad er adressen? *va ehr a-drah-sehn* |

PHRASE BUILDER

| **Where is a ...?** | Hvor er der et ...? | *vor ehr dah it ...* |
|---|---|---|
| **cheap hotel** | billigt hotel | *bee-leet hor-tehl* |
| **good hotel** | godt hotel | *got hor-tehl* |
| **nearby hotel** | hotel i nærheden | *hor-tehl ee nehr-hi-thehn* |

## Fast Talk

### Using Patterns

Look out for patterns of words or phrases that stay the same, even when the situation changes, eg 'Do you have ...?' or 'I'd like to ...'. If you can recognise these patterns, you're already halfway there to creating a full phrase. The dictionary will help you put other words together with these patterns to convey your meaning – even if it's not completely grammatically correct in all contexts, the dictionary form will always be understood.

| Could you write the address, please? | Kunne De skrive adressen ned? pol *koo*-neh dee *sgree*-weh a-*drah*-sehn nith |
|---|---|

## Booking & Checking In

| Do you have any rooms available? | Har I ledige værelser? hah ee *li*-thee *vehrl*-sah |
|---|---|
| How many nights? | Hvor mange nætter? vor *mahng*-eh *neh*-dah |

---

PHRASE BUILDER

| I'd like ... | Jeg vil gerne have ... | yai vi *gehr*-neh ha ... |
|---|---|---|
| a single room | et enkelt-værelse | it *ehng*-gehlt-vehrl-seh |
| a double room | et dobbelt-værelse | it *dob*-ehld-vehrl-seh |
| to share a dorm | plads i en sovesal | plas ee in *so*-we-sahl |
| a bed | en seng | in sehng |

## PHRASE BUILDER

| I'm going to stay for ... | Jeg bliver ... | yai bleeɍ ... |
|---|---|---|
| one day | en nat | in nat |
| two days | to nætter | tor *nehd*-ah |
| one week | en uge | in *oo*-eh |

| | |
|---|---|
| It's ... per day/per person. | Det koster ... per dag/per person. di *kos*-dah ... pehɍ da/pehɍ pehɍ-*sorn* |
| How much is it per night/per person? | Hvor meget koster det per nat/per person? vor *mah*-eth *kos*-dah di pehɍ nat/pehɍ pehɍ-*sorn* . |
| Does it include breakfast? | Er morgenmad inkluderet? ehɍ *morn*-math ing-kloo-*di*-ahth |
| It's fine, I'll take it. | Det er fint, jeg tager det. di ehɍ feent yai tah di |
| I'm not sure how long I'm staying. | Jeg ved ikke hvor længe jeg bliver. yai vith ig vor *lehng*-eh yai bleeɍ |
| Where is the bathroom? | Hvor er toilettet? vor ehɍ toy-*lehd*-eht |
| Is there somewhere to wash clothes? | Er der et sted jeg kan vaske tøj? ehɍ dehɍ it sdehth yai ka vas-geh toy |
| Is there a lift? | Er der elevator? ehɍ dehɍ i-leh-*va*-tor |
| Can I use the kitchen? | Må jeg bruge køkkenet? må yai *bɍoo*-eh *kerk*-neht |

| Can I use the telephone? | Må jeg benytte telefonen?<br>mã yai bi-*ner*-deh ti-leh-*for*-nehn |
|---|---|

| I want a room with a ... | Jeg vil gerne have et værelse med ... | yai vi *gehf*-neh ha it *vehfl*-seh meh ... |
|---|---|---|
| bathroom | bad | bath |
| double bed | dobbeltseng | *do*-behld-sehng |
| shower | brusebad | *bfoo*-seh-bath |
| TV | TV | ti vi |

## Requests & Questions

| Please wake me up at ... | Kunne De vække mig klokken ...? pol<br>*koo*-neh dee *veh*-geh mai *klog*-gehn ... |
|---|---|
| The room needs to be cleaned. | Værelset trænger til at blive gjort rent.<br>*vehfl*-seht *tfaing*-ah ti at blee-weh gyoofd fehnd |
| Please change the sheets. | Vil De venligst skifte sengetøjet? pol<br>vi dee *vehn*-leest *sgeef*-deh *sehng*-eh-toy-yeht |
| I can't open/close the window. | Jeg kan ikke åbne/lukke vinduet.<br>yai ka ig *ãb*-neh/*lã*-geh *vin*-doo-eht |
| I've locked myself out of my room. | Jeg har låst mig ude af værelset.<br>yai hah lãst mai oo-theh a *vehfl*-seht |

34

**The toilet won't flush.** | Toilettet skyller ikke.
toy-*lehd*-deht *sger*-lah ig

## Complaints

**I don't like this room.** | Jeg synes ikke om dette værelse.
yai süns ig om *di*-deh *vehŕl*-seh

PHRASE BUILDER
| **It's (too) ...** | Det er (for) ... | di ehŕ (fo) ... |
|---|---|---|
| **small** | lille | *lee*-leh |
| **noisy** | støjende | *sdoy*-yeh-neh |
| **dark** | mørkt | mergt |
| **expensive** | dyrt | düŕt |

## Checking Out

**I'm/We're leaving now/tomorrow.** | Jeg/Vi rejser nu/i morgen.
yai/vee *ŕai*-sah noo/i morn

**I'd like to pay the bill.** | Jeg vil gerne betale regningen.
yai vi *gehŕ*-neh bi-*ta*-leh *ŕai*-ning-ehn

## Camping

**Am I allowed to camp here?** | Må jeg campere her?
mā yai kahm-*pi*-ah hehŕ

**Is there a campsite nearby?** | Findes der en campingplads i nærheden?
*fin*-ehs dah in *kahm*-ping-plas ee *nehŕ*-hi-thehn

# Eating & Drinking

## ⇒ Fast Phrases

| | | |
|---|---|---|
| Can I see the menu please? | Må jeg se menuen? | må yai si mi-*nü*-ehn |
| I'd like (a beer), please. | Jeg vil gerne have en øl, tak. | yai vil *gehr*-neh ha in erl tahk |
| May I/we have the bill. | Må jeg/vi få regningen? | må yai/vee få *rai*-ning-ehn |

## Meals

| breakfast | morgenmad | *morn*-math |
|---|---|---|
| lunch | frokost | *ffor*-kost |
| dinner | middag/aftensmad | *mi*-da/*ahf*-dehns-math |

## Ordering

| Table for ..., please. | Et bord til ..., tak. |
|---|---|
| | it boof ti ... tahk |

### Fast Talk

**Table Etiquette**

After a meal you should always say Tak for mad (thanks for the meal) before getting up.

## Fast Talk
### Practising Danish

If you want to practise your language skills, try the waiters at a restaurant. Find your feet with straight-forward phrases such as asking for a table and ordering a drink, then initiate a conversation by asking for menu recommendations or asking how a dish is cooked. And as you'll often know food terms even before you've 'officially' learnt a word of the language, you're already halfway to understanding the response.

| | | |
|---|---|---|
| Can I see the menu please? | Må jeg se menuen? | mā yai si mi-*nü*-ehn |
| I'd like the set menu, please. | Jeg tager dagens ret, tak. | yai tah *dah*-ehns faht taht |
| What does it include? | Hvad inkluderer den? | va ing-kloo-*di*-ah dehn |
| Not too spicy please. | Ikke for krydret, tak. | ig fo *krerth*-fahth tahk |

## Special Diets & Allergies

| | | |
|---|---|---|
| I'm a vegetarian. | Jeg er vegetar. | yai ehr veh-geh-*lali* |

### PHRASE BUILDER

| I'd like (the) ..., please. | Jeg vil gerne have ..., tak. | yai vi *geht*-neh ha ... tahk |
|---|---|---|
| bill | regningen | *fai*-ning-en |
| drink list | vinkortet | *veen*-kof-deht |
| menu | menuen | mi-nü-ehn |
| that dish | den ret | den faht |

| I don't eat meat. | Jeg spiser ikke kød. <br> yai *sbees*-ah ig kerth |
| I don't eat chicken, or fish, or pork. | Jeg spiser ikke kylling eller fisk eller svinekød. <br> yai *sbees*-ah ig *kü*-ling *eh*-lah fisk *eh*-lah *svee*-neh-kerth |

## Non-alcoholic Drinks

| apple juice | æblejuice | *eh*-bleh-djoos |
|---|---|---|
| cordial | saftevand | *sahf*-deh-van |
| coffee (with cream) | kaffe (med fløde) | *kah*-feh (meh *fler*-theh) |
| orange juice | appelsinjuice | ah-behl-*seen*-djoos |
| skim milk | skummetmælk | *sgā*-mehth-mehlk |
| soft drink | sodavand | *sor*-da-van |
| carbonated water | danskvand | *dansk*-van |
| tea | te | ti |
| water/ice water | vand/isvand | van/*ees*-van |
| full cream milk | sødmælk | *serth*-mehlk |

## Alcoholic Drinks

| beer/lager | øl | erl |
|---|---|---|
| white wine | hvidvin | *veeth*-veen |
| red wine | rødvin | *ferth*-veen |
| beer | øl/bajer (bajer specifically means a darker beer more like ale, but is used colloquially to mean any beer) | erl/*bay*-yah |

## Fast Talk

### Skål!

When Danes raise their glasses to you and say Skål! it means 'Cheers!', not to be confused with the Australian concept 'to skull', meaning emptying your drink in one go! Also, be prepared to say Skål! a lot more than once during a meal.

## Useful Words

| | | |
|---|---|---|
| **ashtray** | askebæger | *as*-geh-beh-ah |
| **the bill** | regningen | *rai*-ning-ehn |
| **a cup** | en kop | in kop |
| **dessert** | dessert | di-*sehrt* |
| **a drink** | en drink (always alcoholic) | in *dring*-k |
| **a fork** | en gaffel | in *gahf*-ehl |
| **fresh** | fersk/frisk | fehrsk/frehsk |
| **a glass** | et glas | it glas |
| **a knife** | en kniv | in kneew |
| **a plate** | en tallerken | in ta-*lehr*-gehn |
| **spicy** | krydret | *krerth*-rahth |
| **a spoon** | en ske | in ski |
| **stale** | gammel/dårlig | *gah*-mehl/*dor*-lee |
| **sweet** | sød | serth |
| **a teaspoon** | en teske | in *ti*-ski |
| **toothpicks** | tandstikker | *tan*-sdi-gah |

**Pickled...**

Traditional Danish cooking is dominated by, although not to the same extent as the other Scandinavian countries, smoked, cured, pickled or otherwise preserved food, due to the short growing season and long winters. Regional variations are not strong, although proximity to the ocean flavours menus with seafood.

## Staple Foods & Condiments

| | | |
|---|---|---|
| beef | oksekød | *og*-seh-kerth |
| bread | brød | *bŕerth* |
| butter | smør | smer |
| cucumber | agurk | *a-gooŕg* |
| garlic | hvidløg | *vith*-loy |
| meat | kød | kerth |
| mustard | sennep | *seh*-nob |
| mutton | lam | lahm |
| oil | olie | *orl*-yeh |
| pasta | pasta | *pas*-da |
| pepper | peber | *pi*-wah |
| pork | svinekød | *svee*-neh-kerth |
| potatoes | kartofler | kah-*tof*-lah |
| rice | ris | *ŕees* |
| salt | salt | salt |
| sugar | sukker | *sã*-gah |
| veal | kalvekød | *kal*-veh-kerth |
| vegetables | grønsager | *gŕern*-sa-ah |
| vinegar | eddike | *ehth*-geh |

# Menu Decoder

This miniguide to Danish cuisine is designed to help you navigate menus.

## Breakfast Menu

**ost** *åst* cheese
**kaffe** *kah*-feh coffee
**cornflakes** *koorn*-flayks corn flakes
**spejlæg** *spail*-ehg fried egg (always sunny side up)
**frugt** *frågt* fruit
**hårdkogt æg** *hor*-kogt ehg hard-boiled egg
**syltetøj** *sül*-deh-toy jam
**mælk** mehlk milk
**havregryn** *hah*-wah-grün oatmeal
**havregrød** *hah*-wah-grerth porridge
**røræg** *rehr*-ehg scrambled eggs
**blødkogt æg** *blerth*-kogt eht soft-boiled egg
**te** ti tea
**ristet brød/toast** *ris*-deht brer'th/ tawst toast
**yoghurt** *yoo*-goort yoghurt

## Sandwiches

**bøftar tartar** *berf*-ta-tah beef tartar – raw ground beef topped with a raw egg yolk, onion and capers
**dyrlægens natmad** *dür*-leh-ehns *nat*-math 'the veterinarian's midnight snack' – liver paté topped with a thin slice of salt beef, raw onions and beef jelly
**gravad laks** *grah*-wath lahks cured salmon

**leverpostej** *li*-wah-por-sdai liver paté
**marineret sild** mah-ee-*ni*-ath seel pickled herring; served with raw onions
**ostemad** *ås*-deh-math cheese – Denmark is famous for its cheeses, and produces an enormous variety
**rejemad** *rai*-yeh-mahth small shrimp served with mayonnaise and lemon slices
**røget laks** *roy*-yehth lahgs smoked salmon, served with scrambled eggs
**røget sild** *foy*-yehth seel smoked herring on rye bread with chives and a raw egg yolk
**røget ål** *roy*-yehth ål smoked eel, a delicacy
**baguette** *frahns*-brerth franskbrød
**bread** brerth brød
**crusty roll** *fån*-sder-geh rundstykke
**Danish pastry** vee-nah-*brerth* wienerbrød
**rye bread** *foo*-brerth rugbrød
**soft roll** *bol*-eh bolle
**øllebrød** *er*-leh-brerth a smooth beer and bread dish, a bit like porridge, served hot with milk or whipped cream

## Soup

**fiskesuppe** *fis*-geh-så-beh fish soup, usually creamy

**grønsagssuppe** *gŕern*-sas-så-beh vegetable soup

**gule ærter** *goo*-leh *ehŕ*-dah split pea soup served with pork

**hønsekødssuppe** *hern*-seh-kerth-så-beh chicken soup

## Meats

**and** an duck

**engelsk bøf** *ehng*-ehlsk berf steak

**flæskesteg** *flehs*-geh-sdai roast pork

**hakkebøf** *hag*-eh-berf hamburger

**koteletter** ko-deh-*leh*-dah meat chops

**kylling** *kül*-ing chicken

**lammesteg** *lahm*-meh-sdai roast lamb

**oksesteg** *og*-seh-sdai roast beef lamb

**mørbrad** *mer*-bŕath sirloin

**pølse** *perl*-seh sausage

**kalkun** kal-*koon* turkey

## Meat Dishes

**bankekød** *bahng*-geh-kerth similar to Wienerschnitzel

**boller i karry** *bol*-ah ee *kah*-ee meat balls in a curry sauce, served with rice or potatoes

**bøf med løg** berf meh loy hamburger served with fried onions, potatoes and brown gravy

**flæskeæggekage** (*flehs*-geh)-*eh*-geh-ka-eh egg dish with bacon (a bit like an omelette, but made with flour)

**flæskesteg** *flehs*-geh-sdai pork roast with crispy crackling, served with potatoes, brown gravy and pickled cucumbers

**frikadeller** ffi-ga-*dehl*-ah meat patties made of pork, veal and onion served with potatoes, brown gravy, and pickled cucumbers

**fyldt hvidkålshoved** fült *veeth*-kåls-hor-wehth cabbage leaves wrapped around ground beef

**medisterpølse** meh-*dees*-dah-*perl*-seh large fried sausage served with potatoes, brown gravy and pickled cucumbers

**spaghetti med kødsovs** sba-*geh*-dee meh *kerth*-sows spaghetti with ground beef in a tomato sauce

**stegt flæsk med persillesovs** sdehgt flehsk meh pehŕ-*sil*-eh-sows thick slices of fried bacon with potatoes and a white parsley sauce

## Seafood

**fisk** fisk fish

**forel** fo-*fahl* trout

**kogt torsk** kogt torsk poached cod in a mustard sauce served with boiled potatoes

**helleflynder** *hehl*-eh-flün-ah halibut

**kuller** *kool*-ah haddock

**laks** lahks salmon

**rejer** *ŕai*-yah shrimp

**rødspætte** *ŕerth*-sbeh-deh plaice

**søtunge** *ser*-tång-eh sole

**sild** seel herring

**stegt sild** sdehgt seel fried herring served with potatoes and a white parsley sauce

**stegt ål med** sdehgt ål meh

**stuvede kartofler** sdoo-weh-theh kah-*tof*-lah fried eel with boiled potatoes in a white sauce

**torsk** tawsk cod

## Vegetables

**ærter** *ehŕ*-dah peas

**agurk** a-*gooŕk* cucumber

**asparges** a-*sbahŕs* asparagus

**bladselleri** *blath*-si-lah-fee celery

**blomkål** *blom*-kål cauliflower

**broccoli** *bŕo*-kor-lee broccoli

**champignoner** *shahm*-pin-yong-ah mushrooms

**grøn salat** gŕern sa-*lad* lettuce

**gulerødder** *goo*-leh-ŕerth-ah carrots

**kål** kål cabbage

**kartoffel** kah-*tof*-ehl potato
**løg** loy onions
**ris** fees rice
**rødbeder** ferth-*bi*-thah beets (usually served pickled)
**snittebønner** *snee*-deh-bern-ah string beans
**surt/syltede agurker** sooŕt/*sül*-dehthch a-*goof*-ɡah pickled cucumbers
**tomater** to-*ma*-dah tomatoes

## Fruit

**æble** *eh*-bleh apple
**appelsin** ah-behl-*seen* orange
**banan** ba-*nan* banana
**citron** sit-*forn* lemon
**jordbær** yoŕ-behŕ strawberry
**pære** *peh*-fah pear
**vindruer** *veen*-droo-ah grapes

## Desserts

**budding** *boo*-thing a kind of pudding flavoured with, for example, rum or almonds, served warm
**chokoladeis/vanilleis** shor-gor-*la*-theh-ees/va-*neel*-yeh-ees chocolate ice cream/vanilla ice cream
**fromage** ffor-*ma*-sheh a kind of mousse served cold flavoured with, for example, lemon
**jordbær med fløde** yoŕ-behŕ meh fler-thch strawberries with cream
**kage** *ka*-eh cake
**konditorkager** kon-*dee*-dah-ka-ah French pastries
**rødgrød med fløde** forth-gŕerth meh fler-theh fruit pudding (red currant, raspberry, strawberry) served with cream
**pandekager** *pa*-neh-ka-ah crepes rolled around a jam, sugar, or ice cream filling

# Sightseeing & Entertainment

## ⇒ Fast Phrases

| | |
|---|---|
| **When's the museum open?** | Hvornår er museet åbent?<br>vor-*nor* ehr moo-*seh*-eht<br>å-behnt |
| **When's the next tour?** | Hvornår er den næste tur?<br>vor-*nor* ehr dehn *nehs*-deh<br>toor |
| **Can I take photographs?** | Må jeg tage billeder?<br>må yai ta *bil*-thah |

## Sightseeing

| | |
|---|---|
| **Do you (pl) have a guide-book/local map?** | Har I en rejsehåndbog/et lokalkort?<br>hah ee in *rai*-seh-hon-bāw/it lor-*kal*-kort |
| **What are the main attractions?** | Hvad er hovedattraktionerne?<br>va ehr *hor*-wehth-a-*tr*ahg-shorn-ah-neh |
| **What is that?** | Hvad er det?<br>va ehr di |
| **How old is it?** | Hvor gammel er den/det?<br>vor *gah*-mehl ehr dehn/di |

**Fast Talk**

### Forming Sentences

You don't need to memorise complete sentences; instead, simply use key words to get your meaning across. For example, you might know that Hvor means 'where' in Danish. So if you're trying to find a town's castle, just ask Slot hvor? *slot vor*. Don't worry that you're not getting the whole sentence right – people will understand if you stick to the key words.

| How much does it cost to get in? | Hvor meget koster det at komme ind? |
| | vor *mai*-yeht *kos*-dah di at *kom*-eh in |
| What time does it open/ close? | Hvornår åbner/lukker det? |
| | vor-*nor āb*-nah/*lāg*-ah di |

## Sights

| | | |
|---|---|---|
| **beach** | strand | sdŕahn |
| **building** | bygning | *büg*-ning |
| **castle** | slot | slot |
| **cathedral** | katedral/ domkirke | ka-deh-*dŕahl*/ *dom*-keer-g̊en |
| **church** | kirke | *keeŕ*-geh |
| **concert hall** | koncertsal | kon-*sehŕt*-sal |
| **library** | bibliotek | beeb-lee-or-*tĺk* |
| **main square** | hovedtorv | *hor*-wehth-toŕw |
| **market** | marked | *mah*-gehth |
| **mosque** | moské | mor-*ski* |
| **the old city** | den gamle bydel | dehn *gahm*-leh *bü*-dil |
| **opera house** | operahus | *or*-pi-ŕah-hoos |
| **palace** | palads | pa-*las* |

| | | |
|---|---|---|
| **ruins** | ruiner | roo-*een*-ah |
| **stadium** | stadion | *sdad*-yon |
| **university** | universitet | oo-nee-vehŕ-see-*tit* |

## Going Out

| | |
|---|---|
| **What's there to do in the evenings?** | Hvad er der at lave om aftenen? va ehŕ dah o *la*-weh om *ahfd*-nehn |
| **Are there places where you can hear local folk music?** | Findes der steder hvor man kan høre lokal folkemusik? *fin*-ehs dah *sdeh*-thah vor man ka *her*-ah *lor*-kal *fol*-geh-moo-seek |

## Entertainment Venues

| | | |
|---|---|---|
| **cinema** | biograf | bi-or-*gŕahf* |
| **concert** | koncert | kon-*sehŕt* |
| **theatre** | teater | ti-*a*-dah |

46

# Shopping

## ≡ Fast Phrases

| | |
|---|---|
| **Can I look at it?** | Må jeg se den/det?<br>må yai si dehn/di |
| **How much is it?** | Hvor meget koster det?<br>vor *mai*-yeht *kos*-dah di |
| **Can you write down the price?** | Kan du skrive prisen ned?<br>ka doo *sgree*-weh *pree*-sehn nith |

## In the Shop

| | |
|---|---|
| **I'd like to buy ...** | Jeg vil gerne have ...<br>yai vi *gehr*-neh ha ... |
| **Do you (inf) have others?** | Har du andet?<br>hah doo *an*-eht |

### Local Knowledge    Shops

| | |
|---|---|
| **Where would you go for bargains?** | Hvor kan man få gode tilbud?<br>vor ka man få *gor*-thah *til*-booth |
| **Where would you go for souvenirs?** | Hvor kan man købe souvenirs?<br>vor ka man *ker*-beh soo-veh-*neers* |

| | | |
|---|---|---|
| **I don't like it.** | Den/Det kan jeg ikke lide. | dehn/di ka yai ig li |
| **Can I look at it?** | Må jeg se den/det? | mã yai si dehn/di |
| **I'm just looking.** | Jeg kikker bare. | yai *kee*-gah bah |

---

### PHRASE BUILDER

| **Where is a...** | Hvor er der ...? | vor ehŕ dah ... |
|---|---|---|
| **bookshop** | en boghandel | in *bãw*-han-ehl |
| **camera shop** | en fotohandel | in *for*-tor-han-ehl |
| **clothing store** | en tøjbutik | in *toy*-boo-teek |
| **delicatessen** | en delikatesseforretning | in de-lee-ka-*teh*-seh-fo-ŕahd-ning |
| **general store/shop** | en butik | in boo-*teek* |
| **laundry** | et vaskeri | it vas-gah-*fee* |
| **market** | et marked | it *mah*-gehth |
| **newsagency** | en aviskiosk | in a-*vees*-kee-yosk |
| **pharmacy** | et apotek | it ah-por-*tik* |
| **shoeshop** | en skotøjsforretning | *in sgor*-toys-fo-ŕahd-ning |
| **souvenir shop** | en souvenirbutik | in soo-veh-*neeŕ*-boo-teek |
| **supermarket** | et supermarked | it *soo*-bah-mah-gehth |
| **vegetable shop** | en grønthandler | *in gŕernd*-han-lah |

| Can I help you? | Kan jeg hjælpe Dem? pol |
| | ka yai *yehl*-beh dehm |
| Will that be all? | Er det det hele? |
| | ehr di di *hi*-leh |
| Would you like it wrapped? | Ønsker De det pakket ind? pol |
| | *ern*-sgah dee di *pah*-geht in |
| Sorry, this is the only one. | Desværre, dette er den eneste. |
| | dis-*vehr di*-deh ehr dehn i-nehs-deh |
| How much/many do you want? | Hvor meget/mange ønsker De? pol |
| | vor *mai*-yeht/*mahng*-eh *ern*-sgah dee |

## Paying

| How much is it? | Hvor meget koster det? |
| | vor *mai*-yeht *kos*-dah di |
| Do you accept credit cards? | Tager I kreditkort? |
| | tah ee *kreh-deed*-kort |

## Sizes & Comparisons

| small | lille | *lee*-leh |
| --- | --- | --- |
| big | stor | sdoor |
| heavy | tung | tāng |
| light | let | leht |
| more | mere | *mi*-ah |
| less | mindre | *min*-dřah |
| too much/ many | for meget/ mange | fo *mai*-yeht/ *mahng*-eh |
| many | mange | *mahng*-eh |

| enough | nok | nok |
| also | også | os-eh |
| a little bit | en lille smule | in lee-leh smoo-leh |

## Quantities

| a little (amount) | en lille smule | en lee-leh smoo-leh |
| double | dobbelt | dob-ehlt |
| a dozen | et dusin | it doo-seen |
| enough | nok | nok |
| few | få | få |
| less | mindre | min-dřah |
| many | mange | mahng-eh |
| more | mere | mi-ah |
| once | en gang | in gahng |
| a pair | et par | it pah |
| percent | procent | přor-sehnt |
| some | nogle | nor-leh |
| too much | for meget | fo mai-yeht |
| twice | to gange | tor gahng-eh |

## Essential Groceries

| bread | brød | břerth |
| butter | smør | smer |
| milk | mælk | mehlk |
| rice | ris | řees |
| salt | salt | salt |
| shampoo | shampoo | sham-por |
| sugar | sukker | så-gah |

## Local Knowledge

### Shopping

Denmark's many designers and artisans make shopping a delight. Copenhagen is the country's shopping hub, crammed with design shops and indie boutiques, but creativity and first-rate artisanship is on display countrywide.

Besides fashion and accessories, popular purchases include homewares, toys, silverwork, ceramics and hand-blown glass, all in the sleek style that typifies Danish design. Books, foodstuffs and local booze also make fine souvenirs.

| | | |
|---|---|---|
| **toilet paper** | toiletpapir | toy-*lehd*-pah-peef |
| **toothpaste** | tandpasta | *tan*-pas-da |
| **vegetables** | grønsager | *gfern*-sa-ah |

## Souvenirs

| | | |
|---|---|---|
| **earrings** | øreringe | *er*-refing-eh |
| **handicraft** | kunsthåndværk | *kānst*-hon-vehfk |
| **necklace** | halskæde | *hals*-keh-theh |
| **pottery** | keramik | ki-fah *meek* |
| **ring** | ring | fing |
| **rug** | tæppe | *tēh*-beh |

## Clothing

| | | |
|---|---|---|
| **clothing** | tøj | toy |
| **coat** | frakke | *ffah*-geh |
| **dress** | kjole | *kyor*-leh |
| **jacket** | jakke | *yah*-geh |
| **jumper (sweater)** | sweater | *sweh*-dah |

51

| shirt | skjorte | *sgyor*-deh |
|---|---|---|
| shoes | sko | sgor |
| skirt | nederdel | *nith*-ah-dil |
| trousers | bukser | *bāg*-sah |
| It doesn't fit. | Den passer ikke. | dehn pas-ah ig |

PHRASE BUILDER

| It's too ... | Den er for ... | dehn ehŕ fo ... |
|---|---|---|
| big | stor | sdooŕ |
| small | lille | *lee*-leh |
| short | kort | kort |
| long | lang | lahng |
| tight | stram | sdŕahm |
| loose | løs | lers |

## Materials

| cotton | bomuld | *bom*-ool |
|---|---|---|
| handmade | håndlavet | *hon*-la-weht |
| leather | læder | *lehth*-ah |
| brass | messing | *mehs*-sing |
| gold | guld | gool |
| silver | sølv | serl |
| silk | silke | *sil*-geh |
| wool | uld | ool |

## Colours

| black | sort | soŕt |
|---|---|---|

| blue | blå | blå |
|------|-----|-----|
| brown | brun | b́roon |
| green | grøn | ǵrern |
| orange | orange | or-*fang*-sheh |
| pink | rosa | *for*-sa |
| purple | lilla | *li*-la |
| red | rød | ŕerth |
| white | hvid | veeth |
| yellow | gul | gool |

## Toiletries

| comb | kam | kahm |
|------|-----|-----|
| condoms | kondomer | kon-*dorm*-ah |
| deodorant | deodorant | di-or-dor-*ŕahnt* |
| hairbrush | hårbørste | *hor*-bers-deh |
| moisturising cream | fugtigheds-creme | *fåg*-dee-hiths-ḱrehm |
| razor | barberkniv | bah-*biŕ*-kneew |
| sanitary napkins | bind | bin |
| shampoo | shampoo | *shahm*-poo |
| shaving cream | barbercreme | bah-*biŕ*-krehm |
| soap | sæbe | *seh*-beh |
| sunblock cream | solcreme | *sorl*-ḱrehm |
| tampons | tamponer | tahm-*pong*-ah |
| tissues | renseserviet | *ŕahn*-seh-sehŕ-vee-eht |
| toilet paper | toiletpapir | toy-*lehd*-pah-peeŕ |
| toothbrush | tandbørste | *tan*-bers-deh |
| toothpaste | tandpasta | *tan*-pas-da |

## Books & Reading

| map | kort | kort |
|---|---|---|
| **newspaper** | avis | a-*vees* |
| **newspaper in English** | avis på engelsk | a-*vees* på *ehng*-ehlsk |
| **novels in English** | romaner på engelsk | ŕo-*man*-ah på *ehng*-ehlsk |
| **paper** | papir | pa-*peeŕ* |
| **pen (ballpoint)** | kuglepen | *koo*-leh-pehn |
| **scissors** | saks | sahks |

# Practicalities

## ≡ Fast Phrases

| | |
|---|---|
| **Where's the nearest ATM?** | Hvor er den nærmeste hæveautomat? <br> *vor eht dehn ncr-meh-sdeh her-veh-ow-to-maht* |
| **Is there wireless internet access here?** | Er der trådløst internet her? <br> *eht dah trāth-lerst in-tuh-neht hehr* |
| **Where's the toilet?** | Hvor er toilettet? <br> *vor ehr toy-leh-deht* |

## Around Town

| | |
|---|---|
| **What time does it open/close?** | Hvornår åbner/lukker del? <br> *vor-hor āb-nah/lā-gah di* |
| **What street/suburb is this?** | Hvilken gade/forstad er dette? <br> *vil-gehn ga-theh/for-sdath ehr di-deh* |

## Banking

| | |
|---|---|
| **I want to exchange some money.** | Jeg vil gerne veksle nogle penge. <br> *yai vi gehr-neh vehgs-leh nor-leh pehng-eh* |

55

| What is the exchange rate? | Hvad er kursen?<br>va ehr *koor*-sehn |
| How many kroner per dollar? | Hvor mange kroner per dollar?<br>vor *mahng*-eh *kror*-nah pehr *dol*-ah |
| Can I have money transferred here from my bank? | Kan jeg få penge overført hertil fra min bank?<br>ka yai få *pehng*-eh *ow*-ah-fert hehr-*til* frah meen *bahnk* |

---

### PHRASE BUILDER

| I'm looking for ... | Jeg leder efter ... | yai *li*-thah *ehf*-dah ... |
|---|---|---|
| the art gallery | kunstmuseet | *kānst*-moo-seh-eht |
| a bank | en bank | in bahnk |
| the church | kirken | *keer*-gehn |
| the city centre | centrum | *sehn*-trām |
| the ... embassy | den ... ambassade | dehn ... ahm-ba-*sa*-theh |
| my hotel | mit hotel | meet hor-*tehl* |
| a market | et marked | it *mah*-gehth |
| the museum | museet | moo-seh-*eht* |
| the police | politiet | por-lee-tee-*eht* |
| the post office | postkontoret | *post*-kon-tor-eht |
| a public toilet | et offentligt toilet | it o-fehnd-leet toy-*leht* |
| the tourist information office | turist-informationen | too-*reest*-in-for-ma-shor-nehn |

## Fast Talk

### Understanding Danish

Most sentences are composed of several words (or parts of words) serving various grammatical functions, as well as those that carry meaning (primarily nouns and verbs). If you're finding it hard to understand what someone is saying to you, listen out for the nouns and verbs to work out the context – this shouldn't be hard as they are usually more emphasised in speech. If you're still having trouble, a useful phrase to know is Kunne De tale langsommere? *koo-neh dee ta-leh lahng-som-ah?* (Please speak more slowly). The informal version is: Kan du tale langsommere? *ka du ta-leh lahng-som-ah?*

| How long will it take to arrive? | Hvor lang tid vil det tage før de kommer?<br>vor lahng teeth vi di *ta* fer dee *kom*-ah |
|---|---|
| Has my money arrived yet? | Er mine penge kommet?<br>ehr *meen*-eh *pehng*-eh *kom*-eht |

## Useful Words - Banking

| bank draft | bankanvisning<br>*bahnk*-an-vees-ning |
|---|---|
| bank notes | sedler<br>*sehth*-lah |
| cashier | kasserer<br>ka-*si*-ah |
| coins | mønter<br>*mern*-dah |
| credit card | kreditkort<br>*kreh*-*deet*-kort |
| to exchange | at veksle<br>at *vehg*-sleh |

| loose change | småpenge |
|---|---|
| | *smo*-pehng-eh |
| signature | underskrift |
| | *ān*-ah-sgřehft |

## At the Post Office

| I'd like some stamps. | Jeg vil gerne have nogle frimærker. |
|---|---|
| | yai vi *gehř*-neh ha *nor*-leh *ffee*-mehř-gah |
| How much is the postage? | Hvor meget er portoen? |
| | vor *mah*-eth ehř *poř*-tor-ehn? |
| How much does it cost to send this to ...? | Hvor meget koster det at sende dette til ...? |
| | vor *mai*-yeht *kos*-dah di at *sehn*-eh *di*-deh ti ...? |

---

### PHRASE BUILDER

| I'd like to send ... | Jeg vil gerne sende ... | yai vi *gehř*-neh *sehn*-eh ... |
|---|---|---|
| a letter | et brev | it *břeh*w |
| a postcard | et postkort | it *post*-kort |
| a parcel | en pakke | in *pah*-geh |
| a telegram | et telegram | it ti-leh-*gřahm* |
| an aerogram | et aerogram | it eh-for-*gřahm* |

---

## Useful Words - Post

| air mail | luftpost |
|---|---|
| | *lāft*-post |
| envelope | konvolut |
| | kon-vor-*loot* |

| mailbox | postkasse |
| | *post*-ka-seh |
| parcel | pakke |
| | *pah*-geh |
| registered mail | rekommanderet |
| | *řeh*-kom-man-di-ahth |
| surface mail | overfladepost |
| | *ow*-ah-fla-theh-post |

## Phone

| I want to ring ... | Jeg vil gerne ringe til ... |
| | yai vi *gehř*-neh *řing*-eh ti ... |
| The number is ... | Nummeret er ... |
| | *nām*-mahth ehř ... |
| I want to speak for three minutes. | Jeg vil gerne tale tre minutter. |
| | yai vi *gehř*-neh *ta*-leh třeh mee-*noo*-dah |
| How much does a three-minute call cost? | Hvor meget koster det for tre minutter? |
| | vor *mai*-yeht *kos*-dah di fo třeh mee-*noo*-dah |
| How much does each extra minute cost? | Hvor meget koster hvert minut ekstra? |
| | vor *mai*-yeht *kos*-dah vehřt mee-*noot elgs* dřah |
| I'd like to speak to (Mr Pedersen). | Jeg vil gerne tale med (Hr. Pedersen). |
| | yai vi *gehř*-neh *ta*-leh meh (hehř *pih*-dah-sehn) |
| It's engaged. | Der er optaget. |
| | dah ehř *ob*-ta-eht |

| I want to make a reverse-charges phone call. | Jeg ønsker at modtageren skal betale. <br> yai *erns*-gah at *morth*-ta-ahn sga bi-*ta*-leh |
| I've been cut off. | Jeg blev afbrudt. <br> yai bli *ow*-broot |

## Internet

| Where can I get internet access? | Hvor kan jeg få Internet adgang? <br> vor ka yai for *in*-tuh-neht *ath*-guhng |
| I'd like to send an email. | Jeg vil gerne sende en email. <br> yai vil *gehr*-neh *sehn*-neh ehn ee-mayl |
| Do you have wifi? | Har I trådløst netværk? <br> hah ee *tråth*-lerst nehd-verk |
| What's the password? | Hvad er passwordet? <br> va ehr pahs-word-aht |

## Emergencies

| Go away! | Forsvind! <br> fo-s*vin* |
| Help! | Hjælp! <br> yehlp |
| Thief! | Tyv! <br> tüw |
| It's an emergency! | Dette er en nødsituation! <br> *di*-deh ehr en *nerth*-si-too-a-shorn |
| There's been an accident! | Der er sket en ulykke! <br> dah ehr skit in *oo*-ler-geh |

60

| Call a doctor! | Ring efter en læge!<br>ring *ehf*-dah in *leh*-eh |
|---|---|
| Call an ambulance! | Ring efter en ambulance!<br>ring *ehf*-dah in ahm-boo-*lahng*-seh |
| I'm/My friend is ill. | Jeg er/Min ven er syg.<br>yai ehr/meen vehn ehr sü |
| I'm lost. | Jeg er faret vild.<br>yai ehr *fah*-eht veel |
| Where are the toilets? | Hvor er toiletterne?<br>vor ehr toy-*lehd*-dah-neh |
| Could you help me please? | Kan De hjælpe mig? pol<br>ka dee *yehl*-beh mai |
| Could I please use the telephone? | Må jeg låne telefonen?<br>må yai *lā*-neh ti-leh-*for*-nehn |
| I'm sorry. I apologise. | Beklager. Undskyld.<br>bi-*kla*-ah. *ān*-sgül |
| I speak English. | Jeg taler engelsk.<br>yai *ta*-lah *ehng*-elhsg |
| I have medical insurance. | Jeg har sygeforsikring.<br>yai hah *sü*-eh-fo-sig-ring |

PHRASE BUILDER

| I've lost my... | Jeg har mistet ... | yai hah *mis*-deht ... |
|---|---|---|
| bags | min bagage | meen ba-*ga*-sheh |
| handbag | min håndtaske | meen *hon*-tas-geh |
| money | mine penge | *mee*-neh *pehng*-eh |
| passport | mit pas | meet pas |

## Police

| | |
|---|---|
| **I've been raped.** | Jeg er blevet voldtaget. *yai ehr bli*-weht *vol*-ta-eht |
| **I've been robbed.** | Jeg er blevet bestjålet! *yai ehr bli*-weht bi-sdyā-leht |
| **Call the police!** | Ring efter politiet! *ring* ehf-dah por-li-*tee*-eht |
| **Where is the police station?** | Hvor er politistationen? vor ehr por-li-*tee*-sda-shor-nehn |
| **I'll call the police!** | Jeg ringer til politiet! yai *ring*-ah ti por-li-*tee*-eht |
| **I didn't realise I was doing anything wrong.** | Jeg vidste ikke at jeg gjorde noget galt. yai *vis*-deh *ig* at yai *gyor*-eh *nā*-eht gald |
| **I didn't do it.** | Det var ikke mig der gjorde det. di vah ig *mai* dah *gyor* di |
| **I wish to contact my embassy/ consulate.** | Jeg vil gerne kontakte min ambassade/mit konsulat. yai vi *gehr*-neh kon-*tahg*-deh meen ahm-ba-*sa*-theh/meet kon-soo-*lat* |
| **My possessions are insured.** | Mine ejendele er forsikret. *mee*-neh *ai*-ehn-*di*-leh ehr fo-*sig*-faht |
| **My ... was stolen.** | Mit/min... er blevet stjålet. meet/meen ... ehr *bli*-weht *sdyā*-leht |

## Health

| | |
|---|---|
| **I'm sick** | Jeg er syg.<br>yai eh**ŕ** sü |
| **My friend is sick.** | Min ven er syg.<br>meen vehn eh**ŕ** sü |
| **Could I see a female doctor?** | Må jeg få en kvindelig læge?<br>må yai få ın *kvin*-lee *lœh*-eh |
| **What's the matter?** | Hvad er der i vejen?<br>va eh**ŕ** dah ee *vai*-yehn |
| **Where does it hurt?** | Hvor gør det ondt?<br>vor ger di änt |
| **It hurts here.** | Det gør ondt her.<br>di ger änt heh**ŕ** |
| **My ... hurts.** | Min/mit ... gør ondt.<br>meen/meet ... ger änt |

PRACTICALITIES

---

PHRASE BUILDER

| **Where is the ...?** | Hvor er ...? | vor eh**ŕ** ... |
|---|---|---|
| **hospital** | hospitalet | hors-bee-*ta*-leht |
| **chemist** | apoteket | ah-por-*ti*-geht |
| **the casualty ward** | skadestuen | oga-theh-sdoo-ehn |

## Parts of the Body

| | |
|---|---|
| **ankle** | ankel<br>*ahng*-kehl |
| **arm** | arm<br>ahm |
| **back** | ryg<br>ŕerg |

63

| chest | bryst |
| | *bŕerst* |
| ear | øre |
| | *er*-ah |
| eye | øje |
| | *oy*-yeh |
| finger | finger |
| | *fing*-ah |
| foot | fod |
| | forth |
| hand | hånd |
| | hon |
| head | hoved |
| | *hor*-wehth |
| heart | hjerte |
| | *yehŕ*-deh |
| leg | ben |
| | bin |
| mouth | mund |
| | măn |
| ribs | ribben |
| | *ŕee*-bin |
| skin | hud |
| | hooth |
| stomach | mave |
| | *ma*-weh |
| teeth | tænder |
| | *tehn*-ah |
| throat | hals |
| | hals |

## PHRASE BUILDER

| Where is a ...? | Hvor er der en ...? | vor ehŕ dehŕ in ... |
|---|---|---|
| **doctor** | læge | *leh*-eh |
| **dentist** | tandlæge | *tan*-leh-eh |

## Useful Phrases - Health

| | |
|---|---|
| **I'm asthmatic.** | Jeg har astma<br>yai hah *asd*-ma |
| **I'm diabetic.** | Jeg har diabetes<br>yai hah dee-a-*bi*-tehs |
| **I'm epileptic.** | Jeg har epilepsi<br>yai hah eh-pee-lehb-*see* |
| **I'm allergic to antibiotics/penicillin.** | Jeg er allergisk over for antibiotika/penicillin.<br>yai ehŕ a-*lehŕ*-geesk *ow*-ah fo an-tee-bee-*or*-tee-ka/pehn-see-*leen* |
| **I'm pregnant.** | Jeg er gravid.<br>yai ehŕ *gŕah-veeth* |
| **I'm on the pill.** | Jeg bruger p-piller.<br>yai *bŕoo*-ah *pi*-pil lah |
| **I have been vaccinated.** | Jeg er blevet vaccineret.<br>yai ehŕ *bli* wohth vahg-see-*ni*-aht |
| **I have my own syringe.** | Jeg har min egen kanyle.<br>yai hah meen *ai*-yehn ka-*nü*-leh |
| **I feel better/worse.** | Jeg har det bedre/værre.<br>yai hah di *behth*-ah/*vehŕ*-ah |

## PHRASE BUILDER

| I have (a/an) ... | Jeg har ... | yai hah ... |
|---|---|---|
| allergy | allergi | a-lah-*gee* |
| anaemia | anæmi | a-neh-*mee* |
| blister | en vabel | in *va*-behl |
| burn | et brandsår | it *bŕahn*-sor |
| cold | en forkølelse | in fo-*kerl*-seh |
| constipation | forstoppelse | fo-*sdob*-ehl-seh |
| cough | hoste | *hors*-deh |
| diarrhoea | diarré | dee-a-*ŕeh* |
| fever | feber | *fi*-bah |
| headache | hovedpine | *hor*-wehth-pee-neh |
| hepatitis | hepatitis | hi-pa-*tee*-tees |
| indigestion | mavebesvær | *ma*-weh-bi-svehŕ |
| infection | en infektion | in in-fehg-*shorn* |
| influenza | influenza | in-floo-*ehn*-sa |
| lice | lus | loos |
| low/high blood pressure | lavt/højt blodtryk | lowt/hoyt *blorth*-tŕert |
| sore throat | ondt i halsen | ānt ee *hal*-sehn |
| sprain | en forstuvning | in fo-*sdoo*-ning |
| stomachache | ondt i maven | ānt ee *ma*-wehn |
| temperature | feber | *fi*-bah |
| venereal disease | en kønssygdom | in *kerns*-sü-dom |
| worms | orm | oŕm |

## At the Chemist

| | |
|---|---|
| **I need medication for ...** | Jeg skal bruge noget medicin mod ...<br>*yai sga bŕoo-eh nā-eht mi-dee-seen morth ...* |
| **I have a prescription.** | Jeg har en recept.<br>*yai hah in ŕeh-sehbt* |

## At the Dentist

| | |
|---|---|
| **I have a toothache.** | Jeg har tandpine.<br>*yai hah tan-pee-neh* |
| **I've lost a filling.** | Jeg har tabt en plombe.<br>*yai hah tahbt en plām-beh* |
| **I've broken a tooth.** | Jeg har knækket en tand.<br>*yai hah kneh-geht in tan* |
| **My gums hurt.** | Mit tandkød gør ondt.<br>*meet tan-kerth ger ɑnl* |
| **I don't want it extracted.** | Jeg vil ikke have den trukket ud.<br>*yai vi ig ha dehn tŕā-geht ooth* |
| **Please give me an anaesthetic.** | Jeg vil gorno bødøves<br>*yai vi gehŕ-neh bi-der-wehs* |

## Useful Words - Health

| | |
|---|---|
| **accident** | ulykke<br>*oo-ler-geh* |
| **addiction** | afhængighed<br>*ow-hehng-ee-hith* |
| **aspirin** | aspirin<br>*as-bee-ŕeen* |

| | |
|---|---|
| **a bandage** | en bandage<br>in ban-*da*-sheh |
| **blood test** | blodprøve<br>*blorth*-pfer-veh |
| **contraception** | prævention<br>přeh-vehn-*shorn* |
| **medicine** | medicin<br>mi-dee-*seen* |
| **menstruation** | menstruation<br>mins-dřoo-ah-*shorn* |
| **nausea** | kvalme<br>*kval*-meh |
| **oxygen** | oxygen/ilt<br>og-sü-*gin*/eelt |
| **vitamins** | vitaminer<br>vee-ta-*meen*-ah |

## Paperwork

| | |
|---|---|
| **address** | adresse<br>a-*dřah*-seh |
| **age** | alder<br>*al*-ah |
| **birth certificate** | fødselsattest/dåbsattest<br>*fer*-sels-a-tehst/*dābs*-a-tehst |
| **border** | grænse<br>*gřahn*-seh |
| **car registration** | indregistrering (sattest)<br>*in*-řeh-gee-sdřeh-řing (sa-tehst) |
| **customs** | told<br>tol |

68

| | | |
|---|---|---|
| **date of birth** | fødselsdato | *fer*-sehls-da-toh |
| **driver's licence** | kørekort | *ker*-kort |
| **identification** | legitimation | li-gee-tee-ma-*shorn* |
| **immigration** | immigration | i-mee-grah-*shorn* |
| **marital status** | civilstand | see-*veel*-sdan |
| **name** | navn | nown |
| **nationality** | nationalitet | na-shor-na-lee-*tit* |
| **passport** | pas | *pas* |
| **passport number** | pasnummer | *pas*-nam-mah |
| **place of birth** | fødested | *fer*-theh-*sdehth* |
| **profession** | profession | pror-feh-*shorn* |
| **reason for travel** | formål med rejsen | *for*-mål meh *rai*-sehn |
| **religion** | religion | reh-lee-gee-*yorn* |
| **sex** | køn | kern |
| **visa** | visum | *vee*-sam |

# Faroese

*The far-flung Faroes may be under Danish sovereignty, but this self-governing slice of Scandinavia is a universe unto itself. Midway between Iceland and Scotland, it's an 18-piece jigsaw of majestic rocks jutting out of the frothing North Atlantic swells.*

## LANGUAGE

Faroese (often spelled Faeroese) is a twig of the North Germanic branch of the Indo-European tree, which includes Icelandic, Danish, Norwegian and Swedish

★ The population of the Faroe Islands, or Faroes, is about 50,000, which means that Faroese is the mother tongue of only a very small number of people.

★ The Norwegian settlers (about 900 AD) brought their own language to the places they colonised, among them the Faroes, and over the centuries a distinct language developed in the Faroe Islands.

★ The most important factor in the preservation of the language was the oral literature, particularly the kvæði, long epic ballads dealing with ancient legendary characters and events, which are a unique cultural heritage

## HISTORY

Historically the Faroe Islands have been under Norwegian and Danish rule.

★ For several centuries Danish was the dominating language in all administration and in public institutions like schools and the church, and Faroese was degraded to the privacy of the home.

★ In 1846 a Faroese scholar set out to recreate a written norm for Faroese.

★ Today books and newspapers are in Faroese, as are church services and school lessons.

## THE FUTURE

Modern Faroese is under the constant influence of the surrounding world, particularly through the mass media, and there is an ongoing struggle to promote and nourish Faroese in the face of the massive influence of Danish and American English.

## FUN FACTS

★ There are no trains in the Faroe Islands.

★ A Faroese specialty is *skerpikjøt*, mutton which has been wind dried, eaten mostly with bread.

## Numbers

| | | |
|---|---|---|
| 1 | eitt | aitt |
| 2 | tvey | tvuhy |
| 3 | trý | trooi |
| 4 | fýra | fooir-uh |
| 5 | fimm | tim |
| 6 | seks | sehks |
| 7 | sjey | shuhy |
| 8 | átta | ot-tuh |
| 9 | níggju | nooi-djeh |
| 10 | tíggju | tooi-djeh |
| 20 | tjúgu | choo-vu |
| 30 | tretivu | treh-di-veh |
| 40 | fjøruti | fyerr-it-eh |
| 50 | fimmti | fim-ti |
| 60 | seksti | sehks-ti |
| 70 | sjúti | shoo-ti |
| 80 | áttati | waht tuh-ti |
| 90 | níti | nooi-ti |
| 100 | hundrað | hun-druh |

# Faroese Basics

## ≡ Fast Phrases

| Hello. | Halló!/Hey!<br>huh-lloh/huhy |
| --- | --- |
| Thank you. | Takk.<br>tuhk |
| Can you speak English? | Dugir tú eingilskt?<br>du-vir too ain-gilst |

## Essentials

| Yes./No. | Ja./Nei.<br>yae/nai |
| --- | --- |
| Please. | Gerið so væl.<br>djehr-i so vael |
| Thank you. | Takk.<br>tuhk |
| You're welcome. | takka fyri.<br>tuhk-kuh fi-ri |
| Sorry. | Umskylda/Orsaka meg.<br>um-shil-duh/or-saek-i-meh |
| ✂ Excuse me. | Orsaka!<br>or-sae-kuh |

## Language Difficulties

| | |
|---|---|
| **Does anyone speak English?** | Dugir nakar eingilskt? du-vir nae-gar ain-gilst |
| **I (don't) understand.** | Eg skilji (ikki). eh shil-yi (ich-i) |
| **Could you repeat that?** | Kanst tú taka hatta uppaftur? kuhnst too tae kuh huhtt-uh up-uhtt-ur |
| **Could you speak more slowly please?** | Kanst tú gera so væl at tosa seint? kuhns-too djehr-uh so vael uht tos-uh saint |

## Greetings & Introductions

| | |
|---|---|
| **Good morning.** | Góðan morgun. goh-uhn mor-gun |
| **Good afternoon.** | Góðan dag(in). goh-uhn dae(-yin) |
| **Good evening.** | Gott kvøld. gott kverld |
| **Good night.** | Góða nátt. goh-uh nott |
| **What's your name?** | Hvussu eita tú? kvus-seh ai-tuh too |
| **My name is ...** | Eg eiti ... eh ai-ti ... |
| **I'm pleased to meet you.** | Stuttligt at hitta teg. stutt-litt aet hitt-uh teh |
| **How are you?** | Hvussu hevur tú tað? kvus-seh heh-vur too tae |
| **Well, thanks.** | Gott takk. gott tuhk |

**Where are you from?** Hvaðani eru tygum?
kvae-uhn-i ehr-u tiy-un

PHRASE BUILDER

| I'm from .. | Eg eri úr ... | eh ehr-i oor ... |
| --- | --- | --- |
| **Australia** | Avstralia | uhu-strah-li-uh |
| **Canada** | Kanada | kah-nuh-duh |
| **England** | Onglandi | ong-luhn-di |
| **New Zealand** | Nýsælandi | nooi-sae-luhn-di |
| **the USA** | USA | u-ehs-ah |

**Goodbye.** Farvæl.
for-vael

**See you later.** Vit síggjast.
veet sooi-djuhst

## Weather

**What's the weather like?** Hvussu er veðrið?
kvus-seh ehr vehg-reh

**It's ... today.** Veðrið er ... í dag.
vehg-reh ehr ... ooi dae

PHRASE BUILDER

| Will it be ...<br>tomorrow? | Verður tað ...<br>í morgin? | Vehr-ur tae ...<br>ooi mor-djin |
| --- | --- | --- |
| **cold** | kalt | kuhlt |
| **hot** | heitt | haitt |
| **raining** | regn | rehgn |
| **sunny** | sólskin | serl-shin |
| **foggy** | mjørki | myer-ki |

# *Dictionary*

## ENGLISH *to* DANISH

*engelsk – dansk*

Nouns in this dictionary have their gender indicated by Ⓜ or Ⓝ. If it's a plural noun, you'll also see pl. Where a word that could be either a noun or a verb has no gender indicated, it's a verb.

### a

**accommodation** indkvartering *in-kwahr-teh-ring*

**account** konto *kon-toh*

**aeroplane** flyvemaskine *flü-weh-ma-sgee-neh*

**afternoon** eftermiddag *chf-dah-mi-da*

**air-conditioned** air-conditioned *ear-kohn-deh-syond*

**airport** lufthavn *looft-hown*

**airport tax** lufthavnsskat *looft-hown-skat*

**alarm clock** vækkeur *ver-geh-oor*

**alcohol** alkohol *al-koh-horl*

**antique** antik *an-teek*

**appointment** aftale *ow-ta-leh*

**arrivals** ankomst/er *an-kohmst*

**art gallery** kunstgalleri *kånst-gah-luh-ree*

**ashtray** askebæger *as-geh-bea-uh*

**at** ved (location)/klokken (time) *vith/kloh-gehn*

**ATM** hævemaskine *hêr-ve-ma-sgee-neh*

**autumn** efterår *ehf-dah-or*

### b

**baby** baby *bay-bee*

**back (body)** ryg *ferg*

**backpack** rygsæk *ferg-sehk*

**bad** dårlig/t *dor-lee/t*

**bag** taske *tas-geh*

**baggage** bagage *ba-ga-sheh*

75

**baggage allowance** bagage restriktioner ba-*ga*-sheh reh-st*r*ig-*shor*-nah

**baggage claim** bagage afhentning ba-*ga*-sheh ow-hehnt-ning

**bakery** bageri ba-yuh-ree

**Band-Aid** plaster *plas*-tuh

**bank** bank banhk

**bank account** bankkonto *banhk*-kon-toh

**bath** bad bath

**bathroom** badeværelse ba-*theh*-ve*r*l-seh

**battery** batteri ba-dah-*r*ee

**beach** strand sd*r*ahn

**beautiful** smuk/t s*mā*k/t

**beauty salon** skønhedssalon *skern*-hehths-sah-lorng

**bed** seng sehng

**bed linen** sengetøj *sehng*-eh-toy

**bedroom** soveværelse so-veh-*ver*l-seh

**beer** øl erl

**bicycle** cykel *sū*-gel

**big** stor/t sdoo*r*/t

**bill** regning *r*ai-ning

**birthday** fødselsdag *fer*-sels-da

**black** sort sohrt

**blanket** tæppe *ter*-peh

**blood group** blodgruppe *blorth*-g*r*oo-beh

**blue** blå blå

**boarding house** pensionat puhng-sho-*nat*

**boarding pass** boarding pass *bor*-ding-pahs

**boat** båd båth

**book** bog båw

**book (make a booking)** bestille bi-*sdi*-leh

**booked up** alt optaget alt ob-ta-yeht

**bookshop** boghandel *båw*-han-ehl

**border** grænse *gr*ern-seh

**bottle** flaske *flas*-geh

**box** kasse *kas*-eh

**boy** dreng d*r*aing

**boyfriend** kæreste ⓜ/ⓕ *kers*-deh

**bra** brystholder *brers*t-hol-uh

**brakes** bremser *breh*m-sah

**bread** brød *b*ferth

**briefcase** mappe *mah*-beh

**broken** i stykker ee *ster*-gah

**brother** bror *b*foh*r*

**brown** brun *b*roon

**building** bygning *bewg*-ning

**bus (city)** bus boos

**bus (intercity)** regionalbus reh-gyoh-*nahl*-boos

**bus station** busstation boos-sda-shorn

**bus stop** busstop *boos*-sdop

**business** forretning fo-*r*ahd-ning

**business class** business klasse *bis*-nis *klas*-eh

**busy** travl/t t*r*owl/t

**butcher's shop** slagter *slahg*-duh

### C

**cafe** kafe ka-*feh*

**call** opringning ob-*r*ing-ning

**camera** kamera ka-meh-*r*ah

**can (tin)** dåse *dā*-seh

**cancel** afbestille ow-bi-sdi-leh

**car** bil beel

**car hire** billeje *beel*-lai-yeh

**car owner's title** billejer *beel*-lai-yeh-uhn

**car registration** indregistrering *in*-reh-gee-sd*r*eh-ing

**cash** kontanter kon-*tan*-dah

**cashier** kasserer ka-*si*-ah

**chairlift (skiing)** skilift *sgee*-leeft

**change** ændre *ern*-druh

**change (coins)** kontanter kon-*tan*-dah

**change (money)** veksle *vehgs*-leh

**check** checke cheh-keh

**check (banking)** check chehk

**check-in (desk)** indcheckning *in-chehk-ning*

**cheque** check *chehk*

**child** barn *bahrn*

**church** kirke *keer-geh*

**cigarette lighter** lighter *lai-tah*

**city** by *bü*

**city centre** bycenter *bü-sehn-tuh*

**clean** ren/t *rehn/t*

**cleaning** rengøring *rehn-ger-ing*

**cloakroom** garderobe *gah-deh-roh-beh*

**closed** lukket *lâ-geht*

**clothing** tøj *toy*

**coat** frakke *frah-geh*

**coffee** kaffe *kah-feh*

**coins** mønter *mern-dah*

**cold** kold/t *kol/t*

**comfortable** behagelig/t *beh-ha-lee/t*

**company** firma *feer-ma*

**computer** computer *kom-pyoo-duh*

**condom** kondom *kän-dohm*

**confirm (a booking)** bekræfte (en booking) *bi-krahf-deh (en bor-king)*

**connection** forbindelse *fo-bin-ehl-seh*

**convenience store** kiosk *kee-osk*

**cook (chef)** kok *kok*

**cook** lave mad *la-veh math*

**cool** kølig/t *ker-lee/t*

**cough** hoste *hor-sdeh*

**countryside** på landet *på lan-eht*

**cover charge** gebyr *geh-bür*

**crafts** kunsthåndværk *känst-hon-vehrk*

**credit card** kreditkort *kreh-deet-kort*

**currency exchange** valutaveksling *va-loo-ta-vehks-ling*

**customs** told *tol*

## d

**daily** daglig/t *dow-lee/t*

**date** dato *dah-toh*

**date of birth** fødselsdato *fer-sehls-da-toh*

**daughter** datter *da-tah*

**day** dag *da*

**day after tomorrow (the)** i overmorgen *ee ow-ah-morn*

**day before yesterday** i forgårs *ee for-gårs*

**delay** forsinkelse *fo-sing-gehl-seh*

**delicatessen** delikatesser *deh-lee-ka-teh-sah*

**depart** afgå *ow-gå*

**department store** stormagasin *sdoor-mah-ga-seen*

**departure** afgang *ow-gahng*

**deposit** depositum *deh-poh-see-tum*

**diaper** ble *bleh*

**dictionary** ordbog *or-båw*

**dining car** spisevogn *sbee-seh-vown*

**dinner** middag *mi-da*

**direct** direkte *dee-raig-deh*

**dirty** beskidt *bi-sgeet*

**discount** rabat *rah-bal*

**dish** ret *raht*

**doctor** læge *dok-tuh*

**dog** hund *hoon*

**double bed** dobbeltseng *duh-behlt-sehng*

**double room** dobbeltværelse *duh-behlt-vehr-seh*

**dress** kjole *kyor-leh*

**drink** drikke *dri-geh*

**drink (beverage)** drink/drik *drink/drik*

**drivers licence** kørekort *ker-eh-kort*

**drunk** fuld *fool*

**dry** tør/t *ter/t*

## e

**each** hver/t *vehr/t*

**early** tidlig/t *teeth-lee/t*

**east** øst *erst*

**eat** spise *sbee-seh*

ENGLISH *to* DANISH

77

**economy class** økonomiklasse er-koh-noh-*mee*-klas-eh
**elevator** elevator eh-leh-*va*-tor
**embassy** ambassade ahm-ba-*sah*-theh
**English** engelsk *ehng*-ehlsk
**enough** nok nok
**entry** indgang/adgang *in*-gang
**envelope** konvolut kon-voh-*loot*
**evening** aften *ahf*-dehn
**every** hver/t vehr/t
**everything** al/t al/t
**excess (baggage)** overvægt ow-ah-vehgt
**exchange** udveksling (n)/udveksle (v) *ooth*-vehks-ling/*ooth*-vehks-leh
**exhibition** udstilling *ooth*-sti-ling
**exit** udgang *ooth*-gahng
**expensive** dyr/t dür/t
**express (mail)** ekspres ehks-*prehs*

## f

**fall** falde *fal*-eh
**family** familie fa-*mee*-lee-eh
**fare** billetpris bi-*lehd*-prees
**fashion** mode *mor*-theh
**fast** hurtig/t *hoor*-tee/t
**father** far fah
**ferry** færge *fer*-weh
**fever** færre *fer*-eh
**film (for camera)** film feelm
**fine (penalty)** bøde *ber*-theh
**finger** finger *fing*-ah
**first class** førsteklasse *fers*-deh-klas-eh
**fish shop** fiskeforretning *fis*-geh-fo-*fahd*-ning
**fleamarket** loppemarked *lob*-beh-mah-gehth
**flight** fly flü
**floor (storey)** etage eh-*ta*-sheh
**flu** influenza in-floo-*ehn*-suh
**footpath** fortov fo-torw

**foreign** udenlandsk oo-thehn-lansk
**forest** skov skohw
**free (at liberty)** fri free
**free (gratis)** gratis *gfah*-tees
**fresh** frisk/t ffrehsk
**friend** ven/inde vehn/*in*-neh

## g

**garden** have *hah*-veh
**gas (for cooking)** gas gas
**gas** gas gas
**gift** gave *ga*-veh
**girl** pige *pee*-eh
**girlfriend** kæreste ⓕ *kehfs*-deh
**glasses (spectacles)** briller *bfi*-lah
**gloves** handsker *hans*-gah
**go** gå (walk)/tage til (go to) gå/*ta*-yeh ti
**go out** gå ud gå ooth
**go shopping** købe ind *ker*-beh in
**gold** guld gool
**grateful** taknemmelig *tahk*-nehm-lee
**gray** grå gfå
**green** grøn gfern
**grocery** købmand *kefb*-man
**guesthouse** gæstehus/pensionat *geh*-sdeh-hoos/*pahng*-sho-nat
**guided tour** guidet tur *gai*-dehth toor

## h

**half** halv/t hal/t
**handsome** smuk/t smäk/t
**heated** opvarmet *ob*-vah-meht
**help** hjælpe (v) *yehl*-be
**here** her hehf
**highway** motorvej *mor*-tor-vai
**hire** leje *lai*-yeh
**holidays** ferie feh-ree-eh
**honeymoon** hvedebrødsdage/honeymoon *veh*-theh-bferths-da-yeh/ho-nee-moon

78

**hospital** hospital hors-bee-*tal*
**hot** varm/t vahmt
**hotel** hotel hor-*tehl*
**hour** time *tee*-meh
**husband** mand man

## i

**identification** identifikation ee-*dehn*-tee-fee-ka-shorn
**identification card (ID)** ID-kort ee-dee-kort
**ill** syg/t sü/t
**included** inkluderet in-kloo-*deh*-aht
**information** information/oplysninger in-fo-ma-*shorn*/ob-lüs-ning-ah
**insurance** forsikring fo-sig-ring
**intermission** pause *pow*-seh
**Internet cafe** internet kafe in-tuh-*neht* ka-*feh*
**interpreter** oversætter ow-ah-seh-tuh
**itinerary** rute/itinerary roo-teh/ai-teh-neh-*ra*-ree

## j

**jacket** jakke *yah*-geh
**jeans** cowboybukser koh-boy-*bãg*-sah
**jewellery** smykker *smel*-gah
**journey** rejse *rai*-seh
**jumper** trøje *troy*-eh

## k

**key** nøgle *noy*-leh
**kind** venlig *vehn*-lee
**kitchen** køkken *kerk*-gen

## l

**lane** bane *ba*-neh
**large** stor/t sdoor/t
**last (previous)** sidste *sees*-deh

**late** sen/t sehn/t
**later** senere *seh*-neh-uh
**launderette** møntvaskeri *mernt*-vas-geh-ree
**laundry (clothes)** vasketøj vas-geh-*toy*
**leather** læder *lehth*-ah
**leave** forlade fo-*la*-theh
**left luggage (office)** mistet baggage (kontor) *mees*-tehl ba-*ga*-sheh
**letter** brev *brehw*
**lift** løfte (v) *lerf*-deh
**linen (material)** linned *li*-neth
**locked** låst låst
**look for** kigge efter kee-geh *ehf*-dah
**lost** tabt/mistet tabt/*mees*-teht
**lost property office** mistet baggage (kontor) *mees*-teht ba-*ga*-sheh
**luggage** bagage ba-*ga*-sheh
**luggage lockers** baggageopbevaring ba-*ga*-sheh-ob-beh-*vah*-ring
**lunch** frokost *fror*-kost

## m

**mail (postal system)** post post
**make-up** makeup mayk-uhp
**man** mand man
**manager (restaurant, hotel)** manager/chef ma-*na*-djuh/cheht
**map (of country)** (land)kort (*lan*)kort
**map (of town)** (by)kort (*bü*)kort
**market** marked *mah*-gehth
**meal** måltid *mål* tooth
**meat** kød kerth
**medicine (medication)** medicin mi-*dee*-seen
**metro station** metrostation meh-*tro*-sda-shorn
**midday** middag *mi*-da
**midnight** midnat *meeth*-nat
**milk** mælk mehlk
**mineral water** danskvand *dansk*-van
**mobile phone** mobil *mor*-beel

**modem** modem *mor-dehm*
**money** penge *pehng-eh*
**month** måned *må-nehth*
**morning** morgen *mor-ehn*
**mother** mor mor
**motorcycle** motorcykel *mor-tof-sü-gehl*
**motorway** motorvej *mor-tof-vai*
**mountain** bjerg *byehf̆w*
**museum** museum *moo-seh-uhm*
**music shop** musikbutik *moo-seek-boo-teek*

## n

**name** navn nown
**napkin** serviet *sehr-vee-eht*
**nappy** ble bleh
**newsagent** aviskiosk *a-vees-kee-osk*
**newspaper** avis *a-vees*
**next (month)** næste (måned) *nehs-deh*
**nice** rar/t/behagelig/t (comfortable) *f̆ahf̆/t / be-ha-lee/t*
**night** aften/nat *ahf-dehn/nat*
**night out** bytur *bü-toof*
**nightclub** natklub *nat-kloob*
**no vacancy** alt optaget *alt ob-ta-yeht*
**non-smoking** ikke-rygning *ig-rü-ning*
**noon** middag *mi-da*
**north** nord *nof̆*
**now** nu *noo*
**number** nummer *näm-mah*

## o

**office** kontor *kon-tof̆*
**oil** olie *orl-yeh*
**one-way ticket** envejsbillet *in-vais-bi-leht*
**open** åben *åb-ehn*
**opening hours** åbningstider *åb-nings-tee-tha*

**orange (colour)** orange *or-fang-sheh*
**out of order** i stykker *ee sder-gah*

## p

**painter** maler *ma-lah*
**painting (a work)** maleri *ma-la-ree*
**painting (the art)** kunstmaleri *känst-ma-la-ree*
**pants** bukser *bǎg-sah*
**pantyhose** strømpebukser *stf̆erm-beh-bǎg-sah*
**paper** papir *pah-peef̆*
**party** fest fehst
**passenger** passager *pa-sa-shehf̆*
**passport** pas pas
**passport number** pasnummer *pas-nǎm-mah*
**path** sti stee
**penknife** lommekniv *lor-meh-tüw*
**pensioner** pensionist *pahng-sho-neest*
**performance** forestilling *for-sdi-ling*
**petrol** benzin *behn-seen*
**petrol station** benzinstation *behn-seen-sda-shorn*
**phone book** telefonbog *teh-leh-fon-bǎw*
**phone box** telefonboks *teh-leh-fon-boks*
**phone card** telefonkort *teh-leh-fon-kort*
**phrasebook** parlør *pah-lerf̆*
**picnic** picnic *pik-neek*
**pillow** pude *poo-theh*
**pillowcase** pudebetræk *poo-theh-beh-tf̆aik*
**pink** pink/lyserød *pink/lü-seh-ferth*
**platform** platform/perron *plat-form/peh-f̆ong*
**play (theatre)** skuespil *skoo-eh-sbil*
**police officer** politibetjent *por-lee-tee-beh-chent*
**police station** politistation *por-lee-tee-sda-shorn*

**post code** postkode *post*-koh-theh
**post office** postkontor post-kon-*toŕ*
**postcard** postkort *post*-kort
**pound (money, weight)** pund poon
**prescription** recept *ŕeh-sehpt*
**present** gave *ga*-veh
**price** pris prees

# q

**quick** hurtig/t *hoor*-tee/t

# r

**receipt** kvittering kvee-*teh*-ŕing
**red** rød *ŕerth*
**refund** refundering *ŕeh*-foon-*deh*-ŕing
**rent** husleje *hoos*-lai-yeh
**repair** reparere (v) ŕeh-pah-*ŕeh*-ah
**retired** pensioneret pahng-sho-*neh*-uht
**return (v)** vende tilbage vehn-eh ti-*ba*-yeh
**return (ticket)** retur(billet) ŕe-*toor*-bi-leht
**road** vej vai
**robbery** røveri *ŕer*-vuh-ree
**room** værelse *veŕl*-seh
**room number** værelsesnummer *veŕl*-sehs-*nâm*-mah
**route** rute *roo*-teh

# s

**safe** sikker *si*-gah
**sea** hav how
**season** sæson seh-*sorng*
**seat (place)** sæde *seh*-theh
**seatbelt** sikkerhedssele *si*-gah-hehths-*si*-leh
**self service** selvbetjening sehl-bi-*cheh*-ning
**service** service *seh*-vees

**service charge** gebyr geh-*büŕ*
**share** dele (v) *deh*-leh
**shirt** skjorte *sgyor*-deh
**shoe** sko sgor
**shop** forretning/butik fo-*ŕahd*-ning/boo-*teek*
**shopping centre** indkøbscenter in-kerbs-*sehn*-dah
**short (height)** lav/t laow/t
**show** vise (v) *vee*-seh
**shower** brusebad *bŕoo*-seh-bath
**sick** syg sü
**silk** silke *sil*-geh
**silver** sølv serl
**single (person)** single *sing*-gehl
**single room** enkeltværelse *ehng*-gehlt-*veŕl*-seh
**sister** søster sers-dah
**size (general)** størrelse *sderl*-seh
**skirt** skjorte *sgyor*-deh
**sleeping bag** sovepose sor-veh-*poh*-seh
**sleeping car** sovevogn sor-veh-vown
**slide (film)** dias (film) *dee*-as
**smoke** ryge (v) / røg (n) *ŕü*-yeh/ŕoy
**snack** snack snak
**snow** sne sneh
**socks** sokker *sor*-gah
**son** søn sern
**soon** snart snahrt
**south** syd süth
**spring (season)** forår *for*-or
**square (town)** torv torw
**stairway** trappe *tŕa*-beh
**stamp** frimærke *fŕee*-mehr-kah
**stationer's (shop)** papirhandel/kiosk pah-*peeŕ*-han-ehl
**stolen** stjålen/t *styâ*-lehn/t
**stranger** udlænding (foreigner) *ooth*-lehn-ing
**street** gade/vej *ga*-theh/vai
**student** studerende sdoo-*di*-ah-neh
**subtitles** undertitler *ân*-ah-*teet*-lah
**suitcase** kuffert *kâ*-fehrt

81

**summer** sommer *som*-ah
**supermarket** supermarked *soo*-bah-mah-gehth
**surface mail (land)** overfladepost *ow*-ah-fla-theh-post
**surface mail (sea)** overfladepost *ow*-ah-fla-theh-post
**surname** efternavn ehf-dah-*nown*
**sweater** trøje/sweater *troy*-eh/*sweh*-dah
**swim** svømme (v) *sver*-meh
**swimming pool** svømmepøl/swimming pool *sver*-meh-pool/*swi*-ming-pool

## t

**tall** høj/t hoy/t
**taxi stand** taxaholdeplads *tahk*-sa-hor-leh-plas
**teller** bankekspedient (bank) *bahnk*-ehks-pi-dee-*ehnt*
**ticket** billet bi-*leht*
**ticket machine** billetmaskine bi-leht-ma-*sgee*-neh
**ticket office** billetkontor bi-leht-kon-*tor*
**time** tid teeth
**timetable** tidsplan *teeths*-plan
**tip (gratuity)** tip teep
**to** til ti
**today** idag *ee*-da
**together** sammen *sa*-mehn
**tomorrow** imorgen ee-*morn*
**tour** tur *toor*
**tourist office** turistkontor too-*feest*-kon-*tor*
**towel** håndklæde hon-*kler*-theh
**town** by bü
**train station** togstation *täw*-sda-shorn
**transit lounge** transithal *trahn*-*seet*-hal
**travel agency** rejsebureau *rai*-seh-bü-*roh*

**travellers cheque** rejsecheck *rai*-seh-chehk
**trip** rejse/tur *rai*-seh/*toor*
**trousers** bukser *bäg*-sah
**twin beds** enkeltsenge *ehng*-gehlt-*sehng*-eh

## u

**underwear** undertøj *än*-ah-toy

## v

**vacancy** ledige værelser *li*-thee-eh *ve(l*-sah
**vacant** ledig/t *li*-thee/t
**vacation** ferie feh-ree-*eh*
**validate** validere va-lee-*deh*-reh
**vegetable** grøntsag *gfern*-sa
**view** udsigt *ooth*-sigt

## w

**waiting room** venteværelse vehn-deh-*ve(l*-seh
**walk** gå gä
**warm** varm/t vahm/t
**wash (something)** vaske (noget) *vas*-geh (*nä*-eht)
**washing machine** vaskemaskine vas-geh-mas-*gee*-neh
**watch** ur (n) *oor*
**water** vand van
**way** vej (road)/måde (of doing things) vai/*mä*-theh
**week** uge *oo*-eh
**west** vest vehst
**what** hvad va
**when** hvornår vor-*nor*
**where** hvor vor
**which** hvilken/hvilket *vil*-gehn/*vil*-geht
**white** hvid veeth

**who** hvem *vehm*
**why** hvorfor *vor*-for
**wife** kone/hustru *kor*-neh
**wifi** trådløs/t *trath*-lers/t
**window** vindue *veen*-doo
**wine** vin *veen*
**winter** vinter *vin*-dah
**without** uden *oo*-thehn
**woman** kvinde *kvin*-eh
**wool** uld ool

**wrong (direction)** forkert (retning) for-*kehrt* (*rad*-ning)

## y

**year** år *or*
**yesterday** igår *ee*-gor
**youth hostel** ungdomspension *ang*-doms *pahng*-shorn

# Dictionary

## DANISH *to* ENGLISH

*dansk – engelsk*

Nouns in this dictionary have their gender indicated by ⓜ or ⓕ.
If it's a plural noun, you'll also see pl. Where a word that could be
either a noun or a verb has no gender indicated, it's a verb.

### a

**åben** *åb*-ehn open
**åbningstider** *åb*-nings-tee-tha
opening hours
**ændre** *ern*-druh change
**afbestille** ow-bi-sdi-leh cancel
**afgå** ow-gå depart
**afgang** ow-gahng departure
**aftale** ow-ta-leh appointment
**aften** *ahf*-dehn evening
**air-conditioned** ear-kohn-deh-syond
air-conditioned
**al/t** al/t everything
**alkohol** al-koh-*horl* alcohol
**alt optaget** alt ob-ta-yeht no vacancy
**ambassade** ahm-ba-*sah*-theh
embassy
**ankomst/er** *an*-kohmst arrivals

**antik** an-teek antique
**år** or year
**askebæger** *as*-geh-bea-uh ashtray
**avis** a-*vees* newspaper
**aviskiosk** a-*vees*-kee-osk newsagent

### b

**baby** *bay*-bee baby
**bad** bath bath
**båd** båth boat
**badeværelse** ba-theh-*veirl*-seh
bathroom
**bagage** ba-*ga*-sheh baggage/luggage
**bagage afhentning** ba-*ga*-sheh ow-
hehnt-ning baggage claim
**bagage restriktioner** ba-*ga*-sheh reh-
strig-*shor*-nah baggage allowance
**bageri** ba-yuh-ree bakery

**baggageopbevaring** ba-*ga*-sheh-ob-beh-*vah*-ring luggage lockers
**bane** ba-neh lane
**bank** banhk bank
**bankekspedient (bank)** bahnk-ehks-pi-dee-*ehnt* teller
**bankkonto** banhk-kon-toh bank account
**barn** bahrn child
**batteri** ba-dah-fee battery
**behagelig/t** beh-ha-lee/t comfortable
**bekræfte (en booking)** bi-*krahf*-deh (en bor-king) confirm (a booking)
**benzin** behn-*seen* petrol
**benzinstation** behn-*seen*-sda-*shorn* petrol station
**beskidt** bi-*sgeet* dirty
**bestille** bi-*sdi*-leh book (make a booking)
**bil** beel car
**billeje** beel-lai-yeh car hire
**billejer** beel-lai-yeh-uhn car owner's title
**billet** bi-*leht* ticket
**billetkontor** bi-leht-kon-*tor* ticket office
**billetmaskine** bi-leht-ma-sgee-neh ticket machine
**billetpris** bi-*lehd*-prees fare
**bjerg** byehfw mountain
**blå** blå blue
**ble** bleh diaper
**ble** bleh nappy
**blodgruppe** blorth-*gfoo*-beh blood group
**boarding pass** hor-ding-pahs boarding pass
**bøde** ber-theh fine (penalty)
**bog** båw book
**boghandel** båw-han-ehl bookshop
**bremser** bfehm-sah brakes
**brev** bfehw letter
**briller** bfi-lah glasses (spectacles)
**brød** bferth bread
**bror** bfohf brother
**brun** broon brown
**brusebad** bfoo-seh-bath shower

**brystholder** bferst-hol-uh bra
**bukser** båg-sah pants
**bukser** båg-sah trousers
**bus** boos bus (city)
**business klasse** bis-nis klas-eh business class
**busstation** boos-sda-shorn bus station
**busstop** boos-sdop bus stop
**by** bü city/town
**bycenter** bü-sehn-tuh city centre
**bygning** bewg-neh building
**(by)kort** (bü)kort map (of town)
**bytur** bü-toof night out

## c

**check** chehk check (banking)
**check** chehk cheque
**checke** cheh-keh check
**computer** kom-*pyoo*-duh computer
**cowboybukser** koh-boy-båg-sah jeans
**cykel** sü-gel bicycle

## d

**dag** da day
**daglig/t** dow-lee/t daily
**danskvand** dansk-van mineral water
**dårlig/t** dor-lee/t bad
**dåse** då-seh can (tin)
**dato** dah-toh date
**datter** da-tah daughter
**dele (v)** deh-leh share
**delikatesser** deh-lee-ka-*teh*-sah delicatessen
**depositum** deh-*poh*-see-tum deposit
**dias (film)** dee-as slide (film)
**direkte** dee-*faig*-deh direct
**dobbeltseng** duh-behlt-sehng double bed
**dobbeltværelse** duh-behlt-vefl-seh double room
**dreng** dfaing boy
**drikke** dfi-geh drink

85

**drink/drik** drink/drik drink (beverage)
**dyr/t** dür/t expensive

## e

**efterår** ehf-dah-or autumn
**eftermiddag** ehf-dah-mi-da afternoon
**efternavn** ehf-dah-*nown* surname
**ekspres** ehks-*prehs* express (mail)
**elevator** eh-leh-*va*-tor elevator
**engelsk** ehng-ehlsk English
**enkeltsenge** ehng-gehlt-*sehng*-eh twin beds
**enkeltværelse** ehng-gehlt-*verl*-seh single room
**envejsbillet** *in*-vais-bi-leht one-way ticket
**etage** eh-*ta*-sheh floor (storey)

## f

**færge** fer-weh ferry
**færre** fer-eh fever
**falde** fal-eh fall
**familie** fa-*mee*-lee-eh family
**far** fah father
**ferie** feh-ree-eh holidays/vacation
**fest** fehst party
**film** feelm film (for camera)
**finger** fing-ah finger
**firma** feer-ma company
**fiskeforretning** fis-geh-fo-*fahd*-ning fish shop
**flaske** flas-geh bottle
**fly** flü flight
**flyvemaskine** flü-weh-ma-*sgee*-neh aeroplane
**fødselsdag** fer-sels-da birthday
**fødselsdato** fer-sehls-da-toh date of birth
**forår** for-or spring (season)
**forbindelse** fo-*bin*-ehl-seh connection
**forestilling** for-sdi-ling performance
**forkert (retning)** for-*kehrt* (*fad*-ning) wrong (direction)

**forlade** fo-*la*-theh leave
**forretning** fo-*fahd*-ning business
**forretning/butik** fo-*fahd*-ning/boo-*teek* shop
**forsikring** fo-*sig*-fring insurance
**forsinkelse** fo-*sing*-gehl-seh delay
**førsteklasse** fers-deh-klas-eh first class
**fortov** fo-torw footpath
**frakke** ffah-geh coat
**fri** free free (at liberty)
**frimærke** *free*-mehr-kah stamp
**frisk/t** ffehsk fresh
**frokost** fror-kost lunch
**fuld** fool drunk

## g

**gå** gå walk
**gå (walk)/tage til (go to)** gå/*ta*-yeh ti go
**gå ud** gå ooth go out
**gade** *ga*-theh street
**gæstehus** geh-sdeh-hoos guesthouse
**garderobe** gah-deh-*foh*-beh cloakroom
**gas** gas gas (for cooking)
**gas** gas gas
**gave** *ga*-veh gift/ present
**gebyr** geh-*bür* service charge/fee
**grå** gfå gray
**græmse** gfern-seh border
**gratis** *gfah*-tees free (gratis)
**grøn** gfern green
**grøntsag** gfern-sa vegetable
**guidet tur** gai-dehth toor guided tour
**guld** gool gold

## h

**hævemaskine** her-ve-ma-*sgee*-neh ATM
**halv/t** hal/t half
**håndklæde** hon-*kler*-theh towel
**handsker** hans-gah gloves
**hav** how sea

**have** *hah*-veh garden
**her** hehr here
**hjælpe (v)** *yehl*-be help
**høj/t** hoy/t tall
**hospital** hors-bee-*tal* hospital
**hoste** *hor*-sdeh cough
**hotel** hor-*tehl* hotel
**hund** hoon dog
**hurtig/t** *hoor*-tee/t fast/quick
**husleje** *hoos*-lai-yeh rent
**hvad** va what
**hvedebrødsdage/honeymoon** *veh*-thch-*bferths*-da-yeh/*ho*-nee-moon honeymoon
**hvem** vehm who
**hver/t** vehr/t each/every
**hvid** veeth white
**hvilken/hvilket** *vil*-gehn/*vil*-geht which
**hvor** vor where
**hvorfor** *vor*-for why
**hvornår** vor-*nor* when

### i

**i forgårs** ee for-*gårs* day before yesterday
**i overmorgen** ee ow-ah-*morn* day after tomorrow (the)
**i stylkker** ee ster-gah broken/out of order
**idag** ee *da* today
**identifikation** ee-*dehn*-tee-fee-ka-shorn identification
**ID-kort** ee-*dee*-kort identification card (ID)
**igår** ee-*gor* yesterday
**ikke-rygning** *ig*-rü-ning non-smoking
**imorgen** ee-*morn* tomorrow
**indcheckning** *in*-chehk-ning check-in (desk)
**indgang/adgang** *in*-gang entry
**indgangsbillet (to club)** *in*-gahngs-bi-leht cover charge
**indkøbscenter** in-kerbs-*sehn*-dah shopping centre

**indkvartering** *in*-kwahr-teh-ring accommodation
**indregistrering** *in*-reh-gee-sdfreh-ing car registration
**influenza** in-floo*ehn*-suh flu
**information/oplysninger** in-fo-ma-*shorn*/*ob*-lüs-ning-ah information
**inkluderet** in-kloo-*deh*-aht included
**internet kafe** in-tuh-*neht* ka-*feh* Internet cafe

### j

**jakke** *yah*-geh jacket

### k

**kæreste** ⓕ *kehrs*-deh girlfriend
**kæreste** ⓜ/ⓕ *kers*-deh boyfriend
**kafe** ka-*feh* cafe
**kaffe** *kah*-feh coffee
**kamera** ka-meh-*rah* camera
**kasse** *kas*-eh box
**kasserer** ka-*si*-ah cashier
**kigge efter** *kee*-geh *ehf*-dah look for
**kiosk** kee-*osk* convenience store
**kirke** *keef*-geh church
**kjole** *kyor*-leh dress
**klokken** kloh-gehn at (time)
**købe ind** *ker*-beh in go shopping
**købmand** *kerb*-man grocery
**kød** kerth meat
**kok** kok cook (chef)
**køkken** *kerk*-gen kitchen
**kold/t** kol/t cold
**kølig/t** *ker*-lee/t cool
**kondom** kän-*dohm* condom
**kone** *kor*-neh wife
**kontanter** kon-*tan*-dah cash
**kontanter** kon-*tan*-dah change (coins)
**konto** kon-*toh* account
**kontor** kon-*tor* office
**konvolut** kon-voh-*loot* envelope
**kørekort** *ker*-eh-kort drivers licence
**kreditkort** kreh-*deet*-kort credit card

87

**kuffert** *kā*-fehrt suitcase
**kunstgalleri** *kānst*-gah-luh-ree art gallery
**kunsthåndværk** *kānst*-hon-vehŕk crafts
**kunstmaleri** kānst-ma-la-*ree* painting (the art)
**kvinde** *kvin*-eh woman
**kvittering** kvee-*teh*-ŕing receipt

## l

**læder** *lehth*-ah leather
**læge** *dok*-tuh doctor
**(land)kort** (*lan*)kort map (of country)
**låst** låst locked
**lav/t** laow/t short (height)
**lave mad** *la*-veh math cook
**ledig/t** li-*thee*/t vacant
**ledige værelser** li-thee-eh *veŕl*-sah vacancy
**leje** *lai*-yeh hire
**lighter** *lai*-tah cigarette lighter
**linned** li-*neth* linen (material)
**løfte (v)** *lerf*-deh lift
**lommekniv** *lor*-meh-tūw penknife
**loppemarked** lob-beh-*mah*-gehth fleamarket
**lufthavn** *looft*-hown airport
**lufthavnsskat** *looft*-hown-skat airport tax
**lukket** *lā*-geht closed

## m

**mælk** mehlk milk
**makeup** mayk-uhp make-up
**maler** *ma*-lah painter
**maleri** ma-la-*ree* painting (a work)
**måltid** *māl*-teeth meal
**manager/chef** ma-*na*-djuh/chehf manager (restaurant, hotel)
**mand** man husband
**mand** man man
**måned** *mā*-nehth month
**mappe** *mah*-beh briefcase

**marked** *mah*-gehth market
**medicin** mi-*dee*-seen medicine (medication)
**metrostation** meh-tŕo-sda-shorn metro station
**middag** *mi*-da dinner
**middag** *mi*-da midday/noon
**midnat** *meeth*-nat midnight
**mistet** *mees*-teht lost
**mistet baggage (kontor)** *mees*-teht ba-*ga*-sheh left luggage (office)/ lost property office
**mobil** mor-*beel* mobile phone
**mode** *mor*-theh fashion
**modem** *mor*-dehm modem
**mønter** *mern*-dah coins
**møntvaskeri** mernt-*vas*-geh-ree launderette
**mor** mor mother
**morgen** *mor*-ehn morning
**motorcykel** mor-toŕ-sü-gehl motorcycle
**motorvej** mor-tor-vai highway/ motorway
**museum** moo-*seh*-uhm museum
**musikbutik** moo-*seek*-boo-*teek* music shop
**næste (måned)** *nehs*-deh next (month)
**nat** nat night
**natklub** *nat*-kloob nightclub
**navn** nown name
**nøgle** *noy*-leh key
**nok** nok enough
**nord** noŕ north
**nu** noo now
**nummer** *nām*-mah number

## o

**økonomiklasse** er-koh-noh-*mee*-klas-eh economy class
**øl** erl beer
**olie** *orl*-yeh oil
**opringning** ob-ŕing-ning call
**opvarmet** ob-vah-meht heated

**orange** or-*fang*-sheh orange (colour)
**ordbog** *of*-bâw dictionary
**øst** erst east
**overfladepost** ow-ah-fla-theh-post
surface mail (land)
**overfladepost** ow-ah-fla-theh-post
surface mail (sea)
**oversætter** ow-ah-seh-tuh interpreter
**overvægt** ow-ah-vehgt excess
(baggage)

## P

**på landet** på *lan*-eht countryside
**papir** pah-*peef* paper
**papirhandel** pah-*peef*-han-ehl
stationer's (shop)
**parlør** pah-*lerf* phrasebook
**pas** pas passport
**pasnummer** pas-*nârn*-mah passport
number
**passager** pa-sa-*shehf* passenger
**pause** *pow*-seh intermission
**penge** *pehng*-eh money
**pensionat** puhng-sho-*nat* boarding
house
**pensioneret** pahng-sho-*neh*-uht
retired
**pensionist** pahng-sho-*neest*
pensioner
**perron** peh-*rong* platform
**picnic** *pik*-neek picnic
**pige** *pee*-eh girl
**pink** pink pink
**plaster** *plas*-tuh Band-Aid
**platform** *plat*-form platform
**politibetjent** por-lee-*tee*-beh-chent
police officer
**politistation** por-lee-*tee*-sda-shorn
police station
**post** post mail (postal system)
**postkode** *post*-koh-theh post code
**postkontor** post-kon-*tof* post office
**postkort** *post*-kort postcard
**pris** prees price
**pude** *poo*-theh pillow

**pudebetræk** poo-theh-beh-*tfaik*
pillowcase
**pund** poon pound (money, weight)

## r

**rabat** fah-*bat* discount
**rar/t** fahf/t / nice (comfortable)
**recept** feh-*sehpt* prescription
**refundering** feh-foon-*deh*-fing refund
**regionalbus** reh-gyoh-*nahl*-boos bus
(intercity)
**regning** *fai*-ning bill
**rejse** *fai*-seh journey
**rejse/tur** *fai*-seh/toof trip
**rejsebureau** *fai*-seh-bü-*roh* travel
agency
**rejsecheck** *fai*-seh-chehk travellers
cheque
**ren/t** fehn/t clean
**rengøring** *fehn*-ger-ing cleaning
**reparere (v)** feh-pah-*feh*-ah repair
**ret** faht dish
**retur(billet)** fe-*toof*-bi-leht return
(ticket)
**rød** ferth red
**røveri** fer-vuh-*ree* robbery
**rute** *foo*-teh route
**ryg** ferg back (body)
**ryge (v) / røg (n)** fü-yeh/foy smoke
**rygsæk** *ferg*-schk baoltpaolt

## s

**sæde** *seh*-theh seat (place)
**sæson/årstid** seh-*sorng* season
**sammen** sa-mehn together
**selvbetjening** sehl-bi-*cheh*-ning self
service
**sen/t** sehn/t late
**senere** *seh*-neh-uh later
**seng** sehng bed
**sengetøj** *sehng*-eh-toy bed linen
**service** *seh*-vees service
**serviet** sehr-vee-*eht* napkin
**sidste** *sees*-deh last (previous)

**sikker** *si*-gah safe
**sikkerhedssele** *si*-gah-hehths-*si*-leh seatbelt
**silke** *sil*-geh silk
**single** *sing*-gehl single (person)
**skilift** *sgee*-leeft chairlift (skiing)
**skjorte** *sgyor*-deh shirt
**sko** sgor shoe
**skønhedssalon** *skern*-hehths-sah-lorng beauty salon
**skov** skohw forest
**skuespil** *skoo*-eh-sbil play (theatre)
**slagter** *slahg*-duh butcher's shop
**smuk/t** smāk/t beautiful/handsome
**smykker** *smer*-gah jewellery
**snack** snak snack
**snart** snahrt soon
**sne** sneh snow
**sokker** *sor*-gah socks
**sølv** serl silver
**sommer** *som*-ah summer
**søn** sern son
**sort** sohrt black
**søster** *sers*-dah sister
**sovepose** *sor*-veh-*poh*-seh sleeping bag
**soveværelse** *so*-veh-*verl*-seh bedroom
**sovevogn** *sor*-veh-vown sleeping car
**spise** sbee-seh eat
**spisevogn** sbee-seh-vown dining car
**sti** stee path
**stjålen/t** styā-lehn/t stolen
**stor/t** sdoof/t big/large
**stormagasin** sdoof-mah-ga-seen department store
**størrelse** sderl-seh size (general)
**strand** sdfahn beach
**strømpebukser** stferm-beh-*bāg*-sah pantyhose
**studerende** sdoo-*di*-ah-neh student
**supermarked** soo-bah-*mah*-gehth supermarket
**svømme (v)** *sver*-meh swim
**svømmepøl** *sver*-meh-pool swimming pool

**syd** sūth south
**syg** sū sick
**syg/t** sū/t ill

## t

**tabt** tabt lost
**tæppe** *ter*-peh blanket
**taknemmelig** *tahk*-nehm-lee grateful
**taske** *tas*-geh bag
**taxaholdeplads** *tahk*-sa-*hor*-leh-plas taxi stand
**telefonbog** teh-leh-*fon*-bāw phone book
**telefonboks** teh-leh-*fon*-boks phone box
**telefonkort** teh-leh-*fon*-kort phone card
**tid** teeth time
**tidlig/t** *teeth*-lee/t early
**tidsplan** *teeths*-plan timetable
**til** ti to
**time** *tee*-meh hour
**tip** teep tip (gratuity)
**togstation** *tāw*-sda-shorn train station
**tøj** toy clothing
**told** tol customs
**tør/t** ter/t dry
**torv** torw square (town)
**trådløs/t** *trāth*-lers/t wifi
**transithal** tfahn-*seet*-hal transit lounge
**translation** transliteration term
**trappe** tfa-beh stairway
**travl/t** tfowl/t busy
**trøje** tfoy-eh jumper
**tur** toof tour
**turistkontor** too-*feest*-kon-*tof* tourist office

## u

**uden** oo-thehn without
**udenlandsk** oo-thehn-lansk foreign
**udgang** *ooth*-gahng exit

**udlænding (foreigner)** *ooth*-lehn-ing stranger
**udsigt** *ooth*-sigt view
**udstilling** *ooth*-sti-ling exhibition
**udveksling (n)/udveksle (v)** *ooth*-vehks-ling/*ooth*-vehks-leh exchange
**uge** *oo*-eh week
**uld** ool wool
**undertitler** *ăn*-ah-*teet*-lah subtitles
**undertøj** *ăn*-ah-toy underwear
**ungdomspension** *ăng*-doms-*pahng*-shorn youth hostel
**ur (n)** *ooŕ* watch

### *v*

**vækkeur** ver-geh-*ooŕ* alarm clock
**værelse** *veŕl*-seh room
**værelsesnummer** *veŕl*-sehs-*năm*-mah room number
**validere** va-lee-*deh*-reh validate
**valutaveksling** va-*loo*-ta-vehks-ling currency exchange

**vand** van water
**varm/t** vahmt hot/warm
**vaske (noget)** *vas*-geh (*nă*-eht) wash (something)
**vaskemaskine** vas-geh-mas-*gee*-neh washing machine
**vasketøj** vas-geh-*toy* laundry (clothes)
**ved** vith at (location)
**vej** vai road
**veksle** *vehgs*-leh change (money)
**ven/inde** vehn/*in*-neh friend
**vende tilbage** *vehn*-eh ti-*ba*-yeh return (v)
**venlig** *vehn*-lee kind
**venteværelse** *vehn*-deh-*veŕl*-seh waiting room
**vest** vehst west
**vin** veen wine
**vindue** *veen*-doo window
**vinter** *vin*-dah winter
**vise (v)** *vee*-seh show

**Acknowledgments**
**Production Editor** Damian Kemp
**Language Writers** Bergljót av Skardi, Peter A Crozier, Karin Monk,
Birgitte Hou Olsen
**Cover Designer** Fergal Condon
**Cover Researcher** Gwen Cotter
**Book Designer** Katherine Marsh

**Thanks**
Kate Chapman, James Hardy, Indra Kilfoyle, Wibowo Rusli, Angela
Tinson, Juan Winata

**Published by Lonely Planet Global Ltd**
CRN 554153

ISBN - 9781-7-8701-5555
2nd Edition – July 2023
Text © Lonely Planet 2023
**Cover Image** Nyhavn, Copenhagen, Shutterstock/gmlykin©

Printed in China  10 9 8 7 6 5 4 3 2 1

**Contact** lonelyplanet.com/contact

MIX
Paper from
responsible sources
FSC
www.fsc.org  FSC™ C021741

# Index

# 10 Phrases to Get You Talking

| | |
|---|---|
| **Hello.** | Hej/Goddag. inf/pol<br>hai/gor-*da* |
| **Goodbye.** | Hej hej/Farvel. inf/pol<br>hai hai/fah-*vehl* |
| **Please ... (lit. would you be so kind)** | Vær så venlig at ...<br>vehŕ so vehn-lee at ... |
| **Thank you.** | Tak.<br>tahk |
| **Excuse me.** | Undskyld.<br>*ăn*-sgül |
| **Sorry.** | Undskyld/Beklager.<br>*ăn*-sgül/bi-*kla*-ah |
| **Yes.** | Ja.<br>ya |
| **No.** | Nej.<br>nai |
| **I don't understand.** | Jeg forstår ikke.<br>yai fo-sdor ig |
| **How much is it?** | Hvor meget koster det?<br>vor *mai*-yeht *kos*-dah di |